Praise for

BUSINESS MATTERS:

LESSONS IN LEADERSHIP

AND LIFE

The bottom line is this: more critical business lessons are covered in this book than in most under-graduate and even graduate level courses!

Joseph E. Frack
CPA, CGMA, CEO,
Society of Financial Service Professionals

Love and Buxton have written a touching story that feels real, and has great lessons for dealing with the challenges of transitions in the leadership of a family business.

Gerald M. Czarnecki
Chairman & CEO, Deltennium Group, Inc

Amazing book—insightful—forward looking.

Dr. Larry Barton
President, The American College

BIG
SKY
PRESS

Business Matters: Lessons in Leadership and Life

©Diane Ludgate Love & Dickson C. Buxton, 2014

The authors would like to make it clear that this
book is a work of fiction. All characters, events,
and many locations have been made up and any
connections to actual events and/or individuals are
completely coincidental.

ISBN: 978-0615904887

Business Matters:
Lessons in Leadership & Life

*How to navigate
the turbulent waters
of a business crisis*

A business novel by
DIANE LUDGATE LOVE, PhD
&
DICKSON C. BUXTON

BIG
SKY
PRESS

If you believe in yourself and have dedication and pride—and never quit, you'll be a winner. The price of victory is high, but so are the rewards.

Paul Bryant

If you're going through hell, keep going.

Winston Churchill

ACKNOWLEDGEMENTS

SO MANY PEOPLE helped in different ways to get this book off the ground. I'd like to thank Lise McClendon for her guidance and advice from beginning to end. She generously agreed to look over the first hardcopy draft of this story and when I received it back, I noticed she had gone through at least two packages of sticky notes with her comments. I had a lot to learn about writing and Lise's patience and humor helped me to stick with it. Her help was priceless and I am forever grateful.

My special thanks to Bill Miller and Ron Slocum for their assistance with the banking aspect of the story. My interviews with them provided fuel for the storyline. My sincere thanks to Joe Rafferty for his help simplifying the complexities of Employee Stock Ownership Plans.

Thank you to my good friends Larry Dinger, Christina Armond, Abraham, Kipp Webb, Rob Amson, James

Cunningham, Bobby Jones, Al Dufault, Louis Gries, and William Devane for their creative input. Susan Brock taught me everything I know about the Myers-Briggs Type Indicator© and her legacy lives on through me and my work.

Thanks to Craig Johnston, Dick Toomey, Gerry Czarnecki, Joe Wisniewski, and Harold Peterson for their initial book critiques. All of their comments and suggestions were invaluable. And thanks to my forever friend, Anne Vickman, for all her help and for introducing me to Tanya Pai who took this roughly written story and turned it into this final product.

I want to sincerely thank my best friend, my constant source of inspiration and fun, who also happens to be my husband, Steve Love, for his endless hours of listening to me talk about this story and for motivating me to keep on with it. I could not have done this without him. His inspiration and enthusiasm for this story has meant the world to me.

This project would not have been remotely possible without the man I hold in extreme high regard and is my good friend, Dick Buxton. Since meeting Dick in 1997 when I was starting my business, it had been a dream of mine to someday do some kind of business project with him. Back then I never dreamed we would write a book together. I owe so much to Dick and it was an honor, as well as a lot of fun, to work with him. Dick's intellect, humor, experience, stories, and patience made telling this story possible. Thank you for everything, Dick!

Diane Ludgate Love

OUR NATION IS facing a few years of coming to grips with reality. Some of my friends agree with me that living through the great recession was a good thing for America as this will get us back to our roots of hard work and pride in our own accomplishments.

People started to save again; married couples decided who will stay home and raise the kids and who will work one or even two jobs to ride out the economic storm. Some who were unemployed mowed loans, waited tables, cleaned hotel rooms and did odd jobs to make money after unemployment insurance ran out.

Many started their own business so they would not be dependent upon an employer.

Another greatest generation will evolve as everyone starts to take care of themselves and their own families. Adversity, if it doesn't kill you, makes you stronger.

I grew up in the 1930's and early 1940's and have survived many recessions. My father had a successful business that did not survive the last part of the great depression as he had expanded beyond the cash resources of his company and was too dependent upon his bank. He did not create a succession plan when he started a new company and two years later had a severe accident that resulted in liquidation.

At an early age I started another business but was undercapitalized and that company eventually had to be liquidated.

My family business and personal business experience plus many years of business oriented education has helped me counsel other business leaders on how to avoid too much dependence upon continued good times, good health and a good economy.

My author partner, Dr. Diane Ludgate Love, has been a good friend and advisor for over 15 years. She has also helped our associates become more effective group session presenters and our clients resolve critical conflicts.

It has been a delight to help her tell a compelling story of challenges in family leadership succession.

Dickson Buxton

WE WOULD BOTH like to acknowledge the backbone of the American economy — our family owned businesses. They comprise approximately 80–90% of US businesses and range from "mom-n-pop" stores to the likes of Walmart, Ford, and Marriott. Of the Fortune 500 companies, 35% are family owned. The number of family businesses run by women has grown to nearly 40% in the past five years.

US Dept of Commerce research shows that family owned businesses are less likely to lay off employees regardless of financial performance. Family owned businesses employ over 60% of the US workforce and 78% of all new job creation.

Family businesses are economic powerhouses, creating jobs, paying taxes, and helping build vibrant communities across the country. Our hat's are off to them!

Diane & Dick

INTRODUCTION

SEVERAL YEARS AGO I casually mentioned to my husband, Steve, that I wanted to write a book but didn't know where to start. I had an idea for a storyline in my mind, but I didn't know how to begin. He very matter-of-factly said, "That's easy. Call Dick!" And the rest is history.

When I called Dick Buxton to ask if he'd be willing to partner with me on this project he said, "You bet, but only if I don't have to write it!" He had already written several very successful business books and his experience and guidance were much needed. I told him about the concept and storyline and immediately Dick began to come up with one great idea after another. So began our writing project.

The concept of this story came to me a number of years ago. I could vividly see every character in my mind, I knew their personalities, and I could see the office headquarters where the story takes place. The story just started to unfold. There was no specific business in mind as we wrote this story — it was the result of a career working with all types of people, in all types businesses, and observing all types of business problems and situations.

One of the main characters in the book, Charlie Rowe, is from Dick's latest book, *Lessons in Leadership and Life: Secrets of Eleven Wise Men*. It was especially fun to merge the two stories together. That is why we decided to weave "Lessons in Leadership and Life" into the title of this book.

Having lived in Atlanta, I've always had a soft spot in my heart for the South and wanted the story take place there. The story needed the type of business that most people could relate to and one that was open year round. We decided on a nursery/landscape design business.

I learned more about business and myself writing this book than anything I have done so far in my life. It was an exhilarating, grueling, fun, and humbling experience all in one. I was able to incorporate many of the words of wisdom, quotes, and phrases told to me over the years by friends, family members, colleagues, and clients. It was impossible to mention them all in the acknowledgements.

Dick and I have tried to make it as engaging and interesting and entertaining as possible using real-world business scenarios and actual situations we've seen happen in the business world.

I sincerely hope you enjoy our book no matter your line of work or business experience. Most important, I hope this story inspires you with these lessons in leadership and life.

Enjoy!

Diane

I AM NOT AFRAID OF STORMS

FOR I AM LEARNING TO SAIL

MY SHIP.

LOUISA MAY ALCOTT

CHAPTER ONE

AS DANIEL RICHARDS ROLLED OVER IN BED HE heard rain pounding on his bedroom window. "What time is it, anyway?" he thought. The wind was blowing so hard it was slamming the branches of the old oak tree outside his bedroom window against the side of the house—unusual for fall in Atlanta. And what was that ringing? He fumbled around his nightstand for his iPhone, which he finally managed to find on the fourth ring. In the dark he couldn't make out the number. He pressed talk. "Hello," he mumbled, irritated and confused, as he switched on the light next to the bed.

"Mr. Richards? Is this Daniel Richards?" The woman's voice sounded serious, official. A voice that suggested bad news.

"Yeah, this is he. Who's this? What time is it?" he said, still feeling the effects of the gin and tonics he had consumed only hours before.

"It's 2:45, Mr. Richards. My name is Patricia Cunningham, and I'm calling from Saint Thomas Medical Center. It's about your father, Michael Richards."

Hearing his father's name and the name of a hospital together scared him awake. He sat up in bed and grabbed his glasses, squinting at the clock. "I am very sorry to have to tell you this, but your father is in the ICU here," the voice continued. "He has suffered a very serious heart attack, and you need to get here are quickly as possible. He's asking for you."

Dan struggled to make sense of her words. "Dad's in the hospital? A heart attack? When did it happen?"

"We can fill you in on all those details when you get here. We have him stabilized now, but it was a massive heart attack and it's very serious. You need to get here as quickly as you can. He's on the fifth floor, Room 505."

"I can't believe this. Yeah, okay. I'm on my way," Dan said, a bit more coherently, but still feeling dazed. He wanted to ask a million more questions, but he heard the urgency in the nurse's voice. "Tell him I'll be there as soon as I can. I'm on my way right now."

He hung up the phone and threw off the heavy down comforter that covered him. As he stood up, a wave of nausea swept over him thanks to the four gin and tonics he'd had that evening. He glanced over at the empty side of the king-size bed. For a minute he allowed himself to think about how much his life had changed in the past seven months, since Julie broke off their engagement. She told him he'd changed so much she didn't recognize him anymore, and then she was gone. Just like that. The G&Ts were the best way of coping lately.

Branches scraping against the window shook him out of his reverie. Head pounding, he grabbed the old pair of jeans and the Georgia Tech sweatshirt that he'd left in a heap beside the bed. As he bent down to pull on his jeans, Mulligan appeared in the doorway, tail wagging. Dan had rescued the two-year-old black Lab mix from the local shelter when he and Julie first broke up. Now Mully had become his main source of comfort — especially since Dan had taken to avoiding his friends whenever he could.

"Sorry, girl, you have to stay here," he told her, slipping his feet into his worn-out Merrells.

He went into the bathroom and splashed some cold water on his face, then combed his fingers through his dark brown hair, messy from sleep. His eyes were bloodshot. "God, look at you," he said to his reflection. He was six-foot-two, with an athletic build, and on a good day considered himself pretty good-looking, but the dark circles under his eyes made him look older than his thirty-three years.

He threw on his jacket as he ran down the stairs with Mully at his heels. He could feel his heart beating hard.

Dan made sure Mully had plenty of food and water in her room off the kitchen, then headed to his car, hitting the automatic garage door opener. As he started his Jeep Wrangler, he spotted the stack of inventory reports he had brought home from the office the night before on the passenger seat.

Dan had been working at Richards', the nursery business his grandfather had begun and his father now owned, for the past eighteen months, as a buyer and manager in the supplies center, with a handful of people reporting to him. He had met with his father and several other office managers yesterday before leaving the office and had promised to have his reports done first thing in the morning. But instead they sat in his Jeep all night. Lately that had been his MO — committing to doing something and then making excuses when he didn't follow through. A lot of good that MBA from Georgia Tech was doing him now.

Dan pulled out of the long, tree-lined driveway onto the street and into the downpour. He calculated that he would be at the hospital in less than half an hour at this time of night, despite the rain, which his wipers could barely keep up with.

It was difficult to concentrate. He took the corner onto West Paces Ferry Road a bit too fast, and the car swerved on the slick pavement. He kept thinking about seeing his father just yesterday. He'd looked fine at the meeting and had been his normal cantankerous, irritating self. Sure, he'd let himself go a bit since Dan's mother had died three years ago, but a heart attack?

Mike Richards had been the rock of the family business since taking over from his father, Gabriel, as CEO thirty-some years ago. Gabe Richards was a fearless entrepreneur. He started with nothing, scrapped and saved and built the business on sheer hard work and determination. And the business seemed to be in Mike's blood. After high school, he stepped in full time, and father and son worked side by side through highs and lows — all business, as Mike loved to say. This was Gabe's legacy to Mike, and Mike was committed to doing whatever it took to honor that gift — including sacrificing time with his own family.

On the outside, the Richards looked like the perfect family — the handsome couple with their two beautiful children, Dan and Abby. They had all the accoutrements that went with wealth and success — the country club membership, the gorgeous home, cars, luxury vacations, and lots of toys for the kids. But a very few people knew it was much different behind the scenes. Mike Richards lived to work. He missed countless soccer and baseball games, band performances, and recitals as his children were growing up. "Honey, I'm doing this for you and the family," he would rationalize to his wife. "Why do both parents have to be there? We can always catch up after work. I'm with them when they really need me. The kids will understand." But Dan and Abby never really did — even as adults.

As long as Dan could remember he had longed for his father's attention and approval. In high school he made the honor roll consistently, was captain of his tennis and debate teams, and was elected student body president his senior year. People were always telling him he was a natural-born leader. But Mike dismissed Dan's academic accomplishments, saying, "Your grandfather had an eighth-grade education, and look what he accomplished. These grades show you have a head on your shoulders, but they're just grades. You need street smarts." Still today, he'd give Dan the same refrain.

Finally arriving at the hospital, Dan ran from his car into the lobby and spotted directions to the elevator. Hair dripping, soaked to the bone from the pouring rain, he repeatedly slammed the up button until the elevator arrived. "Calm down. It's going to be okay," he whispered to himself, trying to slow his breath. The elevator door opened onto the ICU, and the on-call nurse directed him to room 505. He jogged down the long hallway to his father's room.

He had never felt so alone in his life. His mother had died a few years ago, and his sister Abby, older by three years, lived across the country in San Diego. And he was about to see his father alive for possibly the last time.

Dan tapped on the door of room 505, which was open just a crack; then, steeling his nerves, he stepped into the room. There, in the dimly lit room, he saw his father, always so strong, lying motionless in a hospital bed with tubes and IVs every-where. Mike's face was ashen. A nurse was standing over him, but when she saw Dan she turned to leave the room, giving him a slight, sympathetic smile. "I'll be back in a few minutes to check on him again," she said quietly. "Can I get you any-thing?" Dan just shook his head. It was nearly impossible for him to speak.

After the nurse left the room, Dan just stood there for a moment. Memories swirled through his head. Slowly he took off his rain-soaked coat and hung it behind the door, then pulled the chair from the corner of the room up next to his father's bed. When had things gotten so bad between them? He couldn't recall. For some reason Mike had been hard on his son from the day he began working at the nursery after gradu-ate school. No idea was good enough, no decision ever right.

Dan touched his father's hand gently. "I'm here, Dad," he said. The steady electronic beep of the heart monitor echoed in the background. "Hey, Dad. I'm here. It's Danny. It's going to be okay," he whispered. He leaned in closer, now holding his father's hand, and pleaded, "Can you hear me, Dad? I'm not ready to lose you." The lump in his throat threatened to choke him. He swallowed, then said the words he had always wanted to say to his father. "Dad, I'm so sorry for being such a disappoi—" His voice cracked, and he swallowed hard. "I love you."

Dan felt his father's hand move slightly in his, and a few seconds later Mike Richards's eyes fluttered open. He turned his head, squinting to see his only son in the dim light. He looked as though he was trying to say something, so Dan carefully lifted his ventilator mask.

His father gave him a look he would never forget—a look of sadness and regret, and love. He began to speak. "I…I'm… sorry for…not being a better father to you…Danny," he said.

With astonishing strength, he grasped Dan's hand, and Dan saw tears shining on his cheeks. "I hope…someday you'll…forgive me. I should've done better…"

"Don't talk, Dad," Dan said. "Save your strength. Please. You're going to get better. You're going to get through this. Everybody needs you. I need you." He could hear desperation creeping into his voice.

He could see his father struggling to breathe and held his hand tighter. "I've always…loved you, Danny. I just couldn't… I'm so sorry," Mike wheezed. "It's yours now. Your legacy…" His voice faded.

"No, Dad. Don't leave. Not now," Dan whispered again and again over the steady, flat tone of the heart monitor. He was still holding his father's hand when the on-call nurse came running into the room. She checked his vitals, then turned sympathy-filled eyes on Dan. "I'm so sorry, Mr. Richards," she said. "Your father has passed."

CHAPTER TWO

THE DREARY, GRAY WEATHER DIDN'T STOP HUN-
dreds of people from coming to give their respects to Mike
Richards's family the day of his funeral. Over the years, Mike
and his wife, Henrietta—Rita to family and friends—had given
much to their community. People were in shock they were
both now gone.

During the service, Dan sat next to his eighty-five-year-old
grandmother, trying his best to be strong for her. Mike had
been her only child. He held her small hand throughout the
service, feeling her tiny, frail bones through the skin.

Abby sat on the other side of Grams with her husband and
two children. Dan glanced at her a few times through the
funeral, noticing that she was completely dry-eyed, her beau-

tiful face set in a stony expression. And when once she turned her head and their eyes locked, she looked away immediately. They'd always had an okay relationship though they'd never been very close, but today she seemed to be avoiding him, even trying not to make eye contact. And while she was polite to people expressing their condolences, she gave off a faint air of impatience, like she couldn't wait to leave. Atlanta was no longer her home.

Dan was surprised to see how many people had come from the company. He was especially grateful for the support of his dad's best friend and the chief operating officer of Richards', William Butler. Will had always been like an uncle to Dan, and as the funeral began to wrap up, he stopped by to see him. "Let me know when you're ready to come back to work," he told Dan. "There are a lot of things we need to discuss, but for now, just take care of yourself — I've got things covered." He gave Dan a hug before he left.

Dan looked after him, his mind racing. He couldn't imagine what the company would be like without his father there. Mike had never really talked about retiring. He'd even joked occasionally about dying at his desk someday. And now he was gone.

Just then, another man approached him. About five-eight, with light brown hair capped in a bald spot and dressed in a sober, dark suit, he looked vaguely familiar, but Dan couldn't recall him off the top of his head. He extended his hand, and Dan shook it. "Frank Wilson," the man said. "Vice president of Comstock National Bank. Our bank has been working with the Richards family for many years. I'm very sorry for your loss."

"Thank you," Dan said automatically, assuming he was just another person Mike had done business with coming to pay his respects. He was about to turn away when Frank said, "I have a few things I'd like to discuss with you when you feel up to it, Mr. Richards." He reached into his suit pocket and retrieved a business card, which he handed to Dan. "It's very important that you call me at your earliest convenience." Surprised, Dan merely nodded. "Again, I'm sorry for your loss," Frank said as he walked away. Dan was still staring after him when he heard Abby's voice at his side. "Dan, we need to talk," she said.

⁓

AFTER DRIVING GRAMS BACK TO HER APARTMENT FROM THE funeral, Dan drove to his own house slowly. Exhausted from the events of the past few days, he just wanted to sit in his favorite overstuffed leather chair with a drink and try to wrap his head around what would happen next. As he and Mully sat in the den staring at the logs burning in the fireplace, he ignored his phone ringing from the kitchen and took another long sip of his gin and tonic.

Loud banging at the back door startled him from his thoughts. When he heard the door open, he recalled he'd left it unlocked, and started to get up until he heard a familiar voice. "Dude, why the hell don't you pick up your phone? I've been calling you for two hours. Where are you?" His best friend and college roommate, Vince Burton, strode into view. Six-foot-five, with short, dark hair and an irreverent smile, Vince looked basically the same as he had when Dan and he met in their freshman dorm — save for the slightly receding hairline and a couple extra pounds around his middle. He lived down the street from Dan and worked at a large Atlanta-based engineering firm; his wife, Susan, a professional caterer, was best friends with Julie.

"Geez, man, I was worried about you," Vince said, opening the mini fridge in the den and removing a beer. "It's like you just disappeared at the funeral. I barely got to talk with you. I was standing there talking with Abby and turned to look for you and you were gone." He popped open the beer and took a long swig as he plopped down on the couch.

Dan sighed. "Don't mention her right now, okay? Just don't."

Vince raised his eyebrows. "Why? What's going on?"

Dan took another sip of his G&T and looked at Vince. Then he said out loud what he hadn't told anyone yet. "Abby wants to sell the business," he said. A lump rose in his throat. "She'd barely said two words to me since she and Jonathan and the kids arrived the other day. And then yesterday at the funeral she came up and said we needed to talk. She'd been acting weird from the moment she arrived — all tense and stressed out. I thought it was just because of Dad. But then she just blurted it out. She wants to get rid of the business. As soon as possible."

Vince said nothing, but Dan could feel himself getting more and more upset. "She's already made arrangements for an attorney at Jonathan's law firm to contact me next week." Then he looked away from Vince, and his voice dropped as he said the part that hurt him the worst. "She said that Dad had no confidence in me, and neither does she. That if I take Dad's place as CEO, I'm going to run the business into the ground.

She wants to get out now before the business starts to go down the tubes."

Vince took another long swallow. "Damn. That's unbelievable. She actually said that?"

Dan nodded. "Those were pretty much her exact words. You know she has always resented the family business because of the way it consumed Dad. He never made time for either of us." Vince nodded. Dan added, "She couldn't wait for college so she could get away, and she couldn't move far enough. She's made it clear she's got nothing but bad memories of the place and wants out."

Abby and Mike had been two of a kind — smart, headstrong, and independent, and she could do no wrong in his eyes because of it. Growing up, she got away with murder. Mike's dream was for her to someday work at the business. Instead, she met Jonathan their senior year in college, married him, and moved to La Jolla after graduation. Jonathan was at the top of his graduating class and got a job offer at one of the top law firms in San Diego right out of college. Abby worked part time for a couple of years before starting their family. Now she split her time among caring for their two children, PTA, Junior League, sessions with her personal trainer, and entertaining.

Dan, on the other hand, loved being at the nursery even as a young boy. Some of his best childhood memories were working beside his grandfather outside with the plants and trees. They had a close relationship, and Dan admired him. After grad school Dan looked forward to possibly being the general manager at Richards'. But to his great surprise and disappointment, his father put him in charge of supplies, the smallest and least visible department there.

Even today, Dan often wondered why. He'd excelled in business school, but Mike, who chose not to go to college, loved to remind Dan that higher education didn't guarantee success in the real world. In fact, he even seemed to hold it against Dan, shooting down his ideas, refusing to promote him to a higher management position, even occasionally openly ridiculing him. And with each passing month, Dan felt more and more defeated.

It had taken its toll on his relationship with Julie, too. As time went on, Dan could feel himself losing his enthusiasm and his self-confidence. Julie had begged him to talk to his father, but Dan knew it would have been futile. Still, he struggled on. For better or worse, his loyalty was to the family business, despite the toll it took on his personal life.

"Does Will know anything about this?" Vince asked, jolting Dan back to the present.

"No," Dan replied. "Like I said, she told me this just a few hours ago. I've been sitting here trying to get my head around everything. This is unbelievable."

They continued to talk a bit longer, until Vince's phone buzzed. "That's the wife," he said, glancing at it. "I better go." Then as he stood, he said, "Hang in there, buddy. Maybe we could go out of town next weekend. Drive up to the cabin, do some fishing, get your mind off things." Dan nodded, but his mind was elsewhere. Vince turned to leave. Dan heard the door open and shut as he sat, staring into the fire.

∽

DESPITE HIS OWN DEEP PERSONAL GRIEF, WILL BUTLER HAD HIS bases covered at Richards'. When he heard the news of Mike's death, he had sent out an all-company message announcing the news and attempting to assure everyone that things were being taken care of. In part of the message he wrote:

> We all know what we have to do. Let's keep our eye on the ball and make Mike proud of us. You are all important to this business. As soon as we iron out some of the administrative details, we will let you know. In the meantime, our hearts and prayers are with Mike's family.

He didn't expect Dan at the office for a few days, so he was surprised to hear a knock on his door at 6:45 the Monday after the funeral. He looked up as Dan appeared in the doorway of his office.

"My gosh, Dan, what are you doing here today — and so early in the morning? Why didn't you call and tell me you were coming in?" Will stood up and gave Dan a hug. "Come on in. Sit down."

Dan took a seat in one of the chairs in front of Will's desk. Unsure of where to begin, he glanced around at the walls of Will's office, decorated with an impressive number of awards and plaques from his extensive military and professional career. A widower in his early sixties, Will had a courtly manner and an energy that belied his age. He kept his lean frame immaculately dressed, and this morning was no exception —

his suit was perfectly pressed, his striped tie coordinated to the socks Dan caught a glimpse of above his well-shined shoes.

"How are you, Danny?" he asked, clasping his hands in front of him on the desk.

"I'm okay," Dan said. "I thought about calling you last night, but..." he trailed off.

"Not a problem. This past week has been a tough one for all of us. We're all still in shock, I think," Will said. He paused and looked at the framed photograph on his desk, which showed Mike and him the previous summer at their country club's annual golf tournament. "You know, I never told you this, but the night of that tournament I told Mike that we needed to think about retiring. You can probably imagine what he said. He was one stubborn SOB," he said, a hint of a smile in his voice.

Dan smiled, too. "Tell me about it," he said. He realized this was the first opportunity the two of them had to talk in private since Mike's death. Will had already gone above and beyond his job holding the company together. Clients and employees trusted and respected him, and Dan knew he had the people and communication skills Mike lacked.

"I know we have a lot to talk about regarding the business," Will said now, "but do you think this is the best time?"

"Actually, I think the sooner, the better. Something pretty serious came up the other day." Dan filled him in about Abby's desire to sell the business. Will was quiet for a moment as he ran his fingers through his thick gray hair. "Well, what did you tell her?" he asked finally.

"I told her this wasn't just her decision to make and that we'd discuss it further in a few days," Dan said. "But you've been with this company as long as Dad was CEO. I could really use your help."

Then he told Will about his encounter with Frank Wilson. "Do you know anything about this?" he asked, hoping Will would shrug it off.

But Will nodded. "Remember as I left the funeral I told you there were a lot of things I needed to update you on? Well, that's one of the things. It's about the bank."

Chapter Three

DAN HAD PROMISED TO HAVE LUNCH THAT NOON with Grams, and as he entered the lobby of Spring Creek Assisted Living, the retirement community where she lived, he spotted her sitting on a sofa in the lobby, hands folded in her lap. She looked younger than her eighty-five years, nails painted light pink, white curls fluffed from her weekly trip to the salon. When she saw Dan she smiled and stood up, and he stooped to hug her. "It's so good to see you, Daniel," she said.

They got in the car and headed to Louie's, her favorite cafe, talking about all the old family friends they'd caught up with at the funeral. Although neither brought it up, Dan knew they were both numb with pain from Mike's death. After they'd sat down and ordered their meals—a cobb salad and an iced tea for Grams, a chicken sandwich and a water for Dan—there was a slight lull in the conversation. Seeing his opportunity, Dan asked, "Grams, did Abby mention anything about the business when she was here?"

"No, she didn't," Grams said. "She had her hands pretty full with the children."

"Oh," Dan said.

Then Grams said, "Let me guess — next you're going to tell me she wants to sell the business." Dan looked up, surprised at his grandmother's perceptiveness.

"Abby never felt the connection to the business like you did, Daniel," she said. "It still makes me smile whenever I remember watching you and Gabe outside working in the nursery when you were a little boy. You just loved getting dirty and playing alongside your grandfather as he worked.

"But Abby never showed that interest. After your grandfather passed away and I decided to move out of our home, I wanted to leave it to you and Abby, hoping it might entice her to come back home to stay. I knew Mike and Rita would have no use for it. You both spent so much time there as children, and it was as much your home as ours."

Grams had decided to move from her home about the time Dan and Julie had gotten engaged, and they jumped at the chance to live there. The house was on a big piece of property in a beautiful neighborhood and in great condition. Since Abby had no interest in it, Dan was happy to buy out her portion. Except for updating some of the appliances, he kept the house pretty much the same as when his grandparents lived there, down to the pictures on the walls and the books on the shelves. It seemed fitting, since Dan and Grams had always had such a close relationship. She knew about the tension that frequently sprang up between his father and him, and Dan had gone to her for advice and comfort throughout his childhood and into business school. He wondered whether Grams had ever had that close of a relationship with his dad. Maybe it could help shed some light on the tangled business situation he now found himself in.

As they were finishing their lunch, Dan said, "Grams, there's still something I don't get. Dad buried himself in work even more than usual after Mom died. And you know he was letting himself go — not eating well, not going to the gym regularly as he always had, and more stressed out and edgy.

"This past year I'd occasionally walk into his office and catch him sitting behind his desk looking off in space, deep in thought. Clearly something was bothering him, but he would always say, 'I'm just thinking,' when I asked him what was on his mind. Do you know what might have been going on?"

Instead of answering him directly, Grams asked, "Daniel, did you know your grandfather kept a journal?" Surprised again, Dan shook his head. "I'm the one who encouraged him to start one years ago," Grams said. "Gabe was a very private man, much like your father, and times were hard back then — he didn't want anyone to know the difficulties he was facing starting the business. He thought it was a sign of weakness to talk about such things. He was never good at expressing himself, even to me, so I suggested he write things down. He eventually found it therapeutic — an outlet for his feelings. I know he kept a journal for years."

She continued. "I tried to get your father to start one, too. He and Gabe were so much alike. It's strange, the relationships between parents and their children. Gabe was so tough on

Michael, and I never understood why. Being an only child had to have been difficult for him, too. We wanted more children, but that was just not in the cards. Gabe never thought Michael was ever doing quite enough."

"Whatever happened to the journals, Grams?" Dan asked. She thought for a second, then said slowly, "I don't know, Daniel. They could still be in the house — but I couldn't say for sure."

Then she said, "I do have something else for you, though." She reached into her purse and pulled out an envelope, slightly yellowed and curled at the corners. She handed it to Dan with a smile, saying, "When you find some time, I think you'll enjoy reading this." Still distracted by the idea of his grandfather's journal, Dan gave it just a quick glance before slipping it into his jacket pocket.

After they paid, Dan drove Grams back to Spring Creek. He walked her to her door and gave her another hug. "Chin up, Daniel," she said as she hugged him back, just like she used to say when he was little and upset about something. Feeling oddly comforted, he got back in the car, gave a final wave, and drove away.

～

DAN HAD A NUMBER OF ERRANDS TO RUN THAT EVENING, including stopping by the bank. He decided to go inside that afternoon instead of using the drive-through, on the off-chance that he'd run into Liz, an employee of the bank he'd met a couple of months ago at his gym. They had been on several casual dates before his father passed away, but in the midst of trying to deal with everything he'd neglected to call her.

He asked another teller if she was around and was informed Liz was out at lunch. A tiny bit relieved, Dan thanked him and left, resolving to call her later that week.

Before it got too dark, he took Mully for a walk through the neighborhood. As they traversed the streets, his thoughts were on his grandfather's journals. If they still existed, where could they be?

After a shower and a quick dinner, Dan got a beer from the fridge and walked into the den. The bookshelves held a combination of his books and some from his grandparents' collection. He knew it was a long shot, but he carefully examined each shelf looking for signs of anything resembling a journal. No such luck.

Then he remembered the attic. Grams had asked to leave some of her things there in case he and Abby wanted them someday. He hadn't been up there in years — if the journals were somewhere in the house, that would be the likeliest place.

He got a flashlight from the kitchen and headed upstairs to the hallway between the bedroom and the living room, where the door to the attic was. He had to give it a slight tug, since it hadn't been opened in years. It swung open, and he began climbing the stairs, as Mully scrambled after him. Dan shone the flashlight around until he saw the light switch and flipped it up, revealing stacks of dusty cardboard boxes. He began reading the labels, some in his grandmother's elegant handwriting, some in his own markedly less refined scrawl, as Mully snuffled around enjoying all the new smells. Her wagging tail tipped over a lighter box, and as Dan went over to the corner where she was to replace it, he noticed a small box in the corner labeled, in Grams's handwriting, simply "Gabe."

Could this be what he thought it was? He carefully moved the dusty box out into the open so he could see it better. He gently pulled back the yellowed masking tape from the top and sides of the box, then lifted the folded cardboard on the top. He reached in and took out several black-and-white photographs, some folded papers, a heavy silk bow tie — mementos from Gabe Richards's life. The sense of history in the air was so dense he could almost taste it. Underneath that was a stack of notebooks, some with wrinkled cardboard covers, others leather-bound. On top was a leather book that looked very old, the cover inscribed with his grandfather's initials. Dan bent back the worn brown cover and read on its inside, "This journal belongs to Gabriel Richards."

This is it, Dan thought. He closed the box and took the book down to the den, grabbing another beer on the way. He settled into his chair and opened the book to the first page.

April 15, 1947

This is the most frightening day of my life. I am 25 years old. What am I doing? Uncle David lent me the money to buy the 20-acre parcel on the edge of town near the old Jones place to start a gardening business. I have never shied away from hard work, and I know about gardening and growing plants from my folks. Emily and I have been married for a year now, and we want to start a family. I have to do this. I have no choice. There is no work to be found. I have to make this business work. God help me.

Dan read on. He learned that the original name of the business had been Richards' Gardening Center, and Grams had worked at the new business right up until Michael was born at the end of that year. Gabe wrote on December 21, 1947:

Words cannot describe what it felt like today as I held my son in my arms for the first time. He is so small, so beautiful. We decided to name him Michael Francis after our fathers. Michael Francis Richards. I cannot believe I have a son. I cannot believe I am a father.

Emily had a very tough time with the delivery, and the doctors have a close eye on her but say she will be fine and home by the end of the week. The baby is healthy and strong. I have a son. This feeling is impossible for me to describe.

Dan could not believe what he was actually reading. He learned that since the weather in Georgia was good year round for growing fruits and vegetables, and with the help of the railroad coming right by their property, Gabe had been able to begin transporting produce to New York and Boston within those first several years. This enabled him to build his first large greenhouse and expand more into floral production.

Dan read about how Gabe opened the first retail outlet in 1951 and replaced it with a larger store in 1957. The next year the company established a vehicle service operation and purchased thirty more acres next to the property in order to someday expand.

It was old family lore how at just ten years old, Mike had started working at the business on weekends. His first job was to clean up after his mother and other employees as they created and displayed floral arrangements that could be stored in large coolers in the retail store. Those coolers were a real innovation back then.

As the business continued to grow, Gabe realized there was a need for landscape design and implementation. So in 1960, he changed the name to simply Richards'. He expanded the business into many of the neighboring counties, and nearly everyone in town got their gardening and landscaping supplies at Richards'.

The business had grown and flourished over the years into a multimillion-dollar company with hundreds of employees. Richards' now had one of the top landscape design divisions in the area, a five-state floral retail business, and ten of the largest and most complete greenhouses in the state.

And, Dan read, none of it would have been possible without the close relationship Gabe had with his banker in those early days. Back then, banking was done with a handshake, and they worked together every step of the way, talking at least weekly.

It was getting late, and as much as Dan wanted to keep reading, he felt his eyelids getting heavy. The past couple of weeks had been grueling. He had buried his father, his sister was threatening to sell their business, and he could now be the one responsible for a company he didn't feel emotionally or professionally ready to run. As he lay down in bed and turned off the light on his bedside table, Dan whispered the words written by his grandfather: "God help me."

CHAPTER FOUR

THE NEXT MORNING DAN'S ALARM WENT OFF AT 5:15, and by 6:30 he was pulling into the parking lot of the company headquarters. He knew he had a lot of things to get done, and he wanted to get started as soon as possible. He spotted Will's Acura in the parking lot and pulled in next to him.

He stopped by the office kitchen and filled two large company ceramic cups with coffee, adding two sugars to one and cream to the other, then headed down the hall to Will's office. The door was open, and Dan knocked on the frame. Will was sitting at his computer, and smiled.

"Thanks for coming in so early," he said, as Dan walked in and sat down. "I see you got us coffee. How are you doing this morning?"

"To be honest, I have a rock in the pit of my stomach," Dan admitted. "Losing Dad was tough enough, but the thought of losing this company is killing me. I don't know where we go from here."

Will took a sip of his coffee, then asked, "What do you know about your father's plans for this business?"

"Dad always said he had everything under control and not to worry about it," Dan said. "You know about the stock Abby and I have. I guess I assumed I'd take over someday, but I never knew about anything for sure. And now with Abby making it clear she wants out . . ."

Will gave a slight smile and set down his coffee cup. "Well, I have some things to tell you that just might surprise you. The best place to start is to tell you it was your father's wish that you run this company. Mike knew Abby had no interest in ever being involved in the business. But he wanted to be fair, which is why he gave you and Abby an equal number of voting stock — 49 percent each."

Dan was surprised to hear this. He always thought they each had 50 percent of the voting stock. "Who has the other 2 percent?" he asked.

Will paused briefly, then said, "I do, Dan. Your father gave me the other 2 percent of the voting shares in the event that something like this ever happened. And here we are. He's gone, and Abby wants out. So I have to ask you, Dan — what do you want?"

Dan's mind was reeling again. Why hadn't his father ever told him any of this? If he'd actually wanted Dan to take over someday, why had he kept him so isolated? Why had he not let

Dan be more active in running the company instead of stuck managing a small department? Nothing made any sense.

"I don't get it. Why the hell was all this kept secret?" was all Dan could say, struggling to keep the anger out of his tone.

Will replied, "Your father never wanted you to feel pressured to take over. He knew you wanted the business someday, but he wanted to give you the time to see how things worked here so you could make your decision from an objective point of view, not out of obligation. He wanted you to have the flexibility to leave and go somewhere else if you wanted. It's a lot of responsibility to be the next one in line here."

Dan was having a hard time processing everything, but Will pressed on. "I want you to know everything," he said. "I personally never agreed with Mike's style of dealing with you. He was purposely very hard on you. It was his way of seeing if you had what it took to run a company like this.

"And as long as we're getting all this out in the open, there's something else I want to tell you. A few years ago I asked your father to let me take over as CEO and run the company. My idea was that Mike would stay on as chairman of the board and spend more time with your mother. And then when you came to work for us, I wanted to put you in charge of one of the larger divisions and report directly to me so I could mentor you into a leadership role. I honestly believe that had things gone that way, so many things could have turned out differently. But your father would have nothing to do with it. I respected him, but he could be damn shortsighted and stubborn."

Dan had finally started to absorb some of the information. "So Dad gave you the key to the future of Richards'. If this situation with Abby gets to the point where we need to vote on what's next, it's your vote that will determine where this company goes?"

"Right. Mike was a traditionalist, too. When he and I had this talk some time ago he was at the peak of his life, and the thought of death never crossed his mind in a concrete way. And he was adamant that either you or Abby would take over if he was not around — not me or anyone else."

Will paused for a moment. "That's why I'm asking you what you want. If you truly want to take over this company, it's going to be a long and tough road. This is a big operation and a hell of a lot of responsibility. Up until now you've only been responsible for your small team. If this company goes down on your watch, it's not just the 350 employees here that would be affected; it's the livelihoods of their families, too. This could be the most important decision you'll ever make in your life, Dan. You'll have a huge responsibility not only to everyone here, but to our customers, the community, and your family.

"Not to pile on, but don't forget that the odds are stacked against you. Roughly 30 percent of family-owned businesses survive to the second generation, and just 15 percent to the third. Businesses like this fail for all sorts of reasons — lack of mentoring and succession planning, proper training and education, generational differences. Too many business owners are just like your father was. They think they'll live forever. That's no way to run a business. It's utterly irresponsible, but it happens all the time."

"So where does all this leave us?" Dan asked.

"The ball is in your court now, Dan. I've always believed in you, but this is entirely up to you. I'll support you in whatever you decide. And I won't think any less of you if you decide to sell. Your father wanted this to be your decision and your decision alone. I'm with you no matter what choice you make."

Dan got up and walked over to the large window overlooking the employee parking lot and the newly remodeled greenhouse. Employees had begun arriving for work, and he noticed the smiles and friendly gestures as they greeted one another. He said, "I know for a fact that Grandfather had his challenges when he first started this place. When I was a kid I knew about some of the ups and downs he dealt with here. But he always said it was all worth it because this business was created for making things grow. He was referring to the company, of course, but he also meant the people. He considered the people here as part of the family, too. There are generations of families who have worked here. Hell, I was here following Grandfather and Dad around as soon as I could walk." He smiled at the memory, then bit his lip. Behind him, Will was quiet.

Finally, Dan took a deep breath and turned around to face Will. With more confidence than he felt, he said, "I can't just give up because I'm afraid of a challenge. If the ball is in my court, I want this company. But I can't do this alone. Are you willing to stay on board until I get things going?"

Will had started smiling the moment Dan began to speak. "Of course, I'll stick around to help you," he said. "You have my word that I'll be here to help you through. But don't think you can take your sweet time! I want to retire one of these years." His tone was kind, and he stood up to shake Dan's hand. The decision had been made. Dan would be the next CEO of Richards'. And he was terrified.

"Shall we take a look at your new office, then?" Will asked.

As they stood outside the office of the CEO, another wave of terror washed over Dan. His father had been in this office such a short time ago, and now he was gone. There was so much to process in such a small amount of time. He ran his fingers through his hair and took a deep breath.

Dan and Will walked into Mike Richards's old office, and the voices inside Dan's head raised to a screech: *What are you doing, Dan? You're not ready for this. You're going to fail. You fail at everything you do. No one believes in you. Who are you kidding?*

Feeling slightly ill, Dan walked over and stood behind his dad's old black leather desk chair as Will pulled up a guest chair on the other side. Dan surveyed the contents of the desktop, noticing a picture he never knew his father had — a framed snapshot of the two of them that had been taken the day of Dan's graduation from Georgia Tech. His dad was beaming in the photo. His eyes threatened to well up, and he blinked hard.

"I know you're scared, Dan," Will said. "I don't blame you. But leadership is more of a mindset than it is a title. True leaders know who they are and have confidence in it. That's crucial in order to gain the trust and loyalty of others. They go hand in hand. You cannot have one without the other and be a successful leader."

"I get what you're saying," Dan said looking around the huge office. Then, feeling overwhelmed, he asked, "But, Will, how am I going to do this? Where do I start?"

"It's your attitude at the beginning of any task or situation more than anything else that will determine its successful outcome. One secret I learned years ago that I use even today are the Five Ps of Leadership: positive attitude, purpose with determination, planning, patience, and perseverance — and I think the most imperative point is the first. With the right attitude and belief in yourself, you can do anything."

Dan must have still looked skeptical, because Will said assuringly, "I know you can do this. But more important, you need to know you can do this."

Trying to shake off his doubts, he asked, "Will, would you write up a company announcement saying that I'm taking over Dad's place? Somehow I think it would be better coming from you right now. And I'll call Abby right away, too."

"Of course, I will," Will replied. "I'll have it ready to send out early this afternoon."

As Will stood up to leave, Georgia, the office manager, tapped on the office door. She expressed her condolences to Dan and said she had been looking for him. She handed Dan a stack of papers, on top of which were two pink slips indicating phone messages.

The top message was from Abby's attorney asking Dan to contact him as soon as possible. The second was from their banker, Frank Wilson, also requesting that Dan call him right away.

"Just a minute, Will," Dan called. Will, who had been about to step out the door, turned back toward Dan. "What do I need to know about the situation with the bank?" he asked.

"Come back to my office in an hour and I'll tell you what I know," Will said. "That will give me time to put together what I have so far."

After Will left, Dan tried to concentrate on sorting through the mountains of paperwork on his desk. He felt so out of his element that it seemed like everything was written in Greek.

To make matters worse, he got several emails from various managers asking him whether the rumors swirling around the office — that Dan was taking over as CEO, that the company would be sold immediately, that there would be major cutbacks — were true. Finally Dan shut off his computer, rubbing his temples.

Then his phone rang. It was Will, asking Dan to come to his office. When he arrived, hoping for some good news, he found Will sitting at his desk amid stacks of reports and folders, his brow furrowed.

"Sit down, Dan," he said. "I don't have all the details yet, but as far as I can tell right now, the situation with the bank is a hell of a lot worse than I suspected."

CHAPTER FIVE

DAN HAD JUST STARTED LEAFING THROUGH THE reports on Will's desk when the CFO of Richards', Dan's cousin Jude Perry, strolled into Will's office. Dan looked up to see a shocked look cross Jude's face before he settled his features into a smile.

"Dan, I didn't expect to see you here," he said, crossing the room to shake Dan's hand. Jude and his family had been at the funeral, but Dan hadn't seen Jude since — in the office or otherwise. "Again, we're all so sorry about losing Mike."

Even though Jude and Dan were cousins, they couldn't be more different. Jude was three years older and about five inches shorter than Dan. He'd been a chubby kid, never into sports like Dan and Abby, and now he carried a sizable spare tire around his middle, which strained the buttons of his oxford shirt. Dan and Abby had done their fair share of teasing him at family reunions when they were young — maybe more than their fair share, Dan admitted to himself — and Jude had a kind of perpetual nervousness to him, noticeable in the way his fingernails were chewed down to the quick and how he was constantly fidgeting.

"I talked briefly to Abby at the funeral," Jude continued. "She seemed pretty broken up."

Dan nodded. Then Will said, "We have a lot of fires to put out right now, and Abby is one of them."

Dan filled him in on Abby's plan to sell the business. Her attorney had already contacted Dan in an effort to get the paperwork going.

He'd expected surprise or outrage from Jude, but instead all Jude said was, "Hmm. Interesting."

"But that's not the reason we asked you to join us, Jude," Will said. "I want you to tell us what you know about this bank situation."

"Well, I can tell you it's serious," Jude said. "Mike maintained all the relationships in the company — with the employees, our customers, and our suppliers. This entire business revolved around him, what he knew, and who he knew. And he only gave information on a need-to-know basis."

Jude continued. "Mike had a close business relationship with Steve Giles, the president of Comstock National Bank who retired several years ago. Since then I've been working with Frank Wilson, who's now the vice president of the bank. From what I've been able to piece together, the bottom line is this: Richards' is out of compliance with several of the covenants of our bank loan, and the bank is within their legal rights to pull our loan if they want to — effective immediately."

Glancing at Dan, he said, "Dan, loan covenants are the conditions in which we, the borrowers, must comply in order to adhere with the terms of the loan agree — "

"I know what loan covenants are," Dan interrupted, irritated.

Jude raised one eyebrow slightly and continued. "From what I can tell, the bank had been giving Richards' additional time to get things back on track. That time is just about up. Our line of credit agreement comes up for renewal the first of the year. I don't think the bank is going to be willing to extend it without a cash infusion. But there's no cash."

"No cash?" Will exclaimed. "What do you mean no cash? You're the CFO — how could you see a cash flow problem and not tell us?"

Jude immediately barked back, "You know as well as I do that Mike wasn't one for sharing information. He had his ways of keeping things to himself. He was handling all this, and I had no idea any of this was going on."

Will told Dan to call the bank and, given the present circumstances, stall scheduling a meeting for as long as possible. That would allow them some much-needed time to get their ducks in a row. Will asked Jude to get him everything he had on the bank situation and suggested an update meeting before leaving work.

Jude nodded silently, grabbed his leather notebook and BlackBerry, and walked out of Will's office. Dan, meanwhile, was just trying to process this new round of information. He told Will he needed a quick break and walked to the kitchen down the hallway to get something to drink. As he was about to enter, he heard whispered conversation — and his name.

"I just don't know whether he's capable of taking over the company," said one voice, which Dan recognized as that of J.D. Brown, a longtime Richards' employee.

"He's been running just that tiny team since he got here," added another, whom he thought was Janice Kay. "It seems like Mike didn't have much confidence in him," said another voice — Amy Schultz, Dan recognized. "I couldn't agree more," added Nancy Nelson, who worked in HR.

"I've worked here for 16 years, and I have a lot tied up in this company," said a fifth — which would be Joanne Duncan, Dan knew. He always saw the five of them eating lunch together and showing one another the latest pictures of their grand-children. "Just because he's Mike's son doesn't mean he has Mike's feel for the business — and I don't want all the work I've put into this company over the years to just go down the drain because of it."

Dan's face felt like it was on fire. Was this how bad things were across the office? Was this what people thought of him? He suddenly realized the women were about to exit the kitchen, but before he could move they came out and saw him standing there. Guilty looks appeared on all of their faces, and Janice stuttered, "Oh! Dan. We didn't know you were in the office today. We didn't expect you so soon after..." she trailed off.

The awkwardness was overwhelming. More to break the silence than anything else, Dan lamely said, "Well, as you can see, I am here." He attempted a weak smile, and the women smiled back nervously. "Well, back to work," said Janice, and they continued quickly down the hall. Dan ducked into the kitchen and leaned against the counter, as he heard — or imagined — more whispers trailing down the hallway.

On autopilot, he filled his cup with coffee, made a beeline back to his father's office, and closed the door. He sat down in the black leather desk chair and turned it to look out the window overlooking the garden center, whose original structure was built by his grandfather more than 60 years ago. The parking lot was filling up, and activity was everywhere.

As he sat there, another wave of self-doubt swept over him. Who was he kidding? Maybe Abby was right, after all — the best thing to do would be just to get out.

Just then he heard a tapping at his door. "Come in," he said, turning around. Will entered, a concerned look on his face. "Have you called the bank yet?" he asked. Dan replied that he hadn't. "Good," Will replied. "Why don't you wait for another hour or so, until Jude returns the additional reports I asked for."

"Sure," Dan said. Then Will laid a piece of paper on the desk. "Thought you might want to have a copy of this," he said. It was a printout of the company-wide email Will had sent announcing Dan as CEO of Richards' — which Dan guessed accounted for the conversation he'd overheard in the kitchen. Now there was no turning back from his decision.

Will then added, "After you left my office I called Carolyn Davis in the sales department. Mike always requested the sales numbers at the beginning of each week. He basically handled sales himself, even though Carolyn is the sales manager. You know micromanaging was practically his middle name. Anyway, according to what Carolyn just gave me, our sales figures are way off projections. Basically, Dan, each department is off by at least 30 percent, with the exception of the floral retail division. We have to look into all this and find out exactly what's going on here."

It wasn't even the end of Dan's first day, and the problems were piling up as high as the reports on his desk. Despite everything, by late afternoon he had moved most of his things to his father's old office on the third floor. And he managed to move the meeting with the bank to the end of the week, giving them time to prepare — a minor success, but an important one.

That afternoon Dan arranged for a neighbor to come by to feed Mully and take her for her evening walk. He wanted to stay late to go through the piles of folders and papers left by his father and organize the endless phone messages to be returned to suppliers and customers to thank them for their kind words and support.

He was packing up his things to leave for the night when he glanced again at the picture on the desk of his dad and him. He sank heavily back into the chair as the enormity of the situation hit him all over again. His parents were gone. The employees of his company, and even his own sister, didn't believe in him. What if the company failed because of his lack of experience? He needed help. *Why didn't you prepare me for this, Dad?* he thought, with his emotions ranging somewhere between anger and regret.

"Hey, are you still here? It's late. Let's get out of here," Dan heard Will's friendly voice coming down the empty hall between their offices. Dan quickly tried to compose himself as Will walked into his office, but he didn't quite succeed.

"I'm sorry to barge in. I didn't realize…" Will said apologetically when he saw Dan's face.

Dan shook his head. "Will, I don't know about any of this. I know I told you this morning I wanted to do this, but I'm in way over my head. I need help. A lot of it," he said regaining his composure.

"I know," Will said. "This has to be overwhelming for you. Who wouldn't be, after all you've been through lately? I've been thinking a lot about all this today, and I have someone in mind who might be able to help you through this. Her name is Michelle Montgomery."

Will sat down as he continued. "She's one of the best executive coaches I know and a savvy business consultant — compassionate but tough, and really results-oriented. I've personally worked with Michelle off and on for several years, and working with her has been one of the best things I've ever done for my professional life.

"I cannot say enough good things about this woman, Dan. She is one of the best in the business. I think you should give her a call and at least talk to her," he said as he pulled a business card out of his pocket and handed it to Dan.

"Executive coach?" Dan said doubtfully as he examined the card, which read "Michelle Montgomery — Executive Coach" in simple black letters. "Will, I need help to keep this business afloat — not someone to critique my résumé. Plus I can't afford to spend money right now for something like that!"

"Can you afford not to?" Will asked. "You don't want to step over dollars to pick up dimes."

"What do you mean? I'm not following you," Dan said.

"You have to look at your future and ask yourself whether your future and the future of this company are worth investing in. I told you I'll be here to help you, but my plate is full.

You need a professional who can help you restore your life and get you back in the game again. You've got to get control of your life, and Michelle can help you do it. She can help you create a plan for rebuilding your life and help you find your self-confidence again."

Will explained that an executive coach was like having a confidential thought partner — someone who always has your best interests at heart. "She helped me refine my leadership style, understand my colleagues better, and be more organized and proactive. She also helped me handle some interpersonal situations with employees and suppliers, and taught me how to polish my professional image and presentational style. She even helped me understand how to control my temper that used to erupt from time to time.

"It boils down to this, Dan. Michelle can help guide you in the direction you want to go, and she'll have your back every step of the way. You do the work, and she's there to observe, ask questions, and hold you accountable for doing what you say you will. The question I'll ask you again is this: Can you afford not to at least try this?"

Exhausted and drained from the day, Dan thanked Will for the suggestion and promised he'd think about it.

Will nodded and stood. Then he said, "Just remember this, Dan. It's from part of a poem I memorized years ago, and I think it holds the secret to successfully navigating through what life tosses at us. 'Keep your head about you even though others are losing theirs and blaming it on you. Trust yourself when others doubt you.' You will get through this if you keep your head about you. It's like I told you this morning — it's your attitude and belief in yourself that will ultimately determine whether you succeed or if you fail. And all of this is completely within your control."

They left the office together, and as they were walking to their cars, Dan stopped and asked, "Will, could I ask you a rather unusual question?"

"Sure. What is it?"

"You and Dad knew each other pretty well. Did he ever say anything to you about any journals — like maybe Grandfather's journals?"

"How do you know about those?" Will asked, sounding a bit taken aback.

Dan explained how he had found one of them.

After a brief pause, Will said, "Yes. I know about the journals. If you don't have to get home right away, maybe we should grab a drink. I told you this morning I wanted to get everything out in the open, and these journals are part of it."

CHAPTER SIX

WILL SUGGESTED THEY STOP FOR A BEER AT Ducey's, a favorite bar near the office, before heading home.

After the waitress brought their drinks, Will took a large sip. Setting it down with a sigh, he said, "Your father was a complicated guy, Dan. Your grandfather was tough on him. Mike found the journals by accident a long time ago. Your grandfather carelessly left one open on his desk, never expecting anyone would come into his den. But one day when Mike was in his twenties and visiting, he needed something from the desk in the den — so he went in and saw the open journal. He read your grandfather's unedited thoughts about the business, his life — and him. And it crushed him."

Will paused for a moment, then said, "Mike was an affable guy and knew a lot of people but had no real close friends. He had an edge about him, too. Who knows why? I think part of it was because of reading that damn journal. He was never the same after reading it. He couldn't get over what his father thought about him."

Resisting the urge to ask what exactly the journal had said, Dan asked, "Did Dad ever confront Grandfather about what he'd read?"

"No. To my knowledge I was the only person he ever told about it, and he made me swear to secrecy. Mike knew what the journals looked like, so periodically when he would check on their house when they were out of town, he'd take one off the shelf and read it. Your grandfather kept them hiding in plain sight in his den. Pretty ballsy if you ask me."

Dan agreed and said, "I found some of Grandfather's journals the other night."

"So you know what's in them, too?" Will asked.

"I've only read part of the first one, but I could tell that Grandfather was determined to make the business successful," Dan said.

"Your grandfather wanted Mike to be just like him and didn't realize, like many uncommon people who found companies, that they cast a long shadow," Will said. "Sons and daughters of self-made successful men and women grow up in that shadow and are in awe of them unless their mother or father becomes a friend and teacher. One-on-one serious conversations can help a son or daughter understand that their parents are human and can make mistakes. Too bad Gabe couldn't have been a little more transparent with Mike, and let him know how he had to face his own demons."

The idea of demons struck Dan. He'd never thought before about how they could be passed down through generations. He remembered when he was a senior in high school and had won captain of the varsity tennis team. He'd gone home so excited, imagining the look of warm approval in his dad's eyes when he shared the news. Instead, Mike had challenged him to a match, right then and there. They drove to the court in the dark, and when Dan finally beat him, Mike said he'd just gotten lucky.

Perhaps guessing the drift of Dan's thoughts, Will said, "I honestly believe, Dan, that your grandfather tried his best to teach Mike — just like Mike tried to do his best with you, in his own way. In the end, we all just want to know we're appreciated and respected…and loved."

As they were leaving Ducey's, Dan said goodbye to Will, then got in his car, lost in thought. Maybe Will was right — maybe he did need to consult a professional about what to do next. He reached into the center console and pulled out Michelle Montgomery's business card. He decided he'd call her after all.

$\approx$

THE NEXT MORNING WHEN DAN GOT TO THE OFFICE, HE TOOK out Michelle's business card again. Even though he still wasn't sure what an executive coach could actually do for him, he thought at this stage he really didn't have much to lose. He picked up the phone and dialed. To his surprise, she answered her own phone on the second ring.

"Dr. Montgomery, this is Dan Richards," Dan said. "I work with William Butler. He gave me your name."

"Ah, yes, Will told me you might be in touch. Please call me Michelle. What can I do for you?" she said

Dan briefly explained his situation and said he didn't know much about executive coaching. "That's no problem," Michelle said. "Perhaps it would be most helpful if we meet to discuss what I do in further detail."

"Are you free for lunch today?" Dan asked. She said she was, and they arranged to meet at noon at an Italian spot downtown.

After he hung up the phone, Dan pulled up Michelle's website. The "About Me" section listed her credentials, which were certainly impressive: PhD, a big-name client base, extensive work history and experience, and several published books and articles. He then noticed a section called "Why Executive Coaching?" and clicked on it. One sentence jumped out at him immediately: "Approximately 40 percent of newly promoted executives and managers fail within 18 months of starting new positions."

Dan continued reading. The next section said:

Here are six questions to ask yourself to see whether executive coaching could work for you:

1. Are there things you could be doing better or differently in your current role (or future role) to be more effective and successful, and could you use some help defining them and getting there?
2. Are there aspects of your life you want to change and want a trusted professional to help you make it happen?

3. Are you ready to find that ideal work/life balance, and to learn to put yourself first to achieve greater alignment between who you are and what you do?
4. Are there specific areas you want to improve that could bring you greater satisfaction and sense of accomplishment?
5. Are you willing to stop or change behaviors that interfere with your personal or professional growth?
6. Are you willing to commit to doing what it takes to make those positive changes in your life?

Dan thought about those questions as he drove to the restaurant. He walked in and scanned the tables, recognizing Michelle from her picture on her website. He nodded to the host and headed to the table, and she stood up to greet him as she saw him approach. She was taller than he expected, about five-foot-eight, and appeared to be in her forties, dressed in a stylish navy-blue suit, with shoulder-length dark brown hair.

"It's very nice to meet you, Dan," she said, shaking his hand. "I'm sorry to hear about your father. I had the pleasure of meeting him last year at a fundraiser for St. Thomas Medical Center. He'll be missed in the community."

"Yes, both my parents were involved with St. Thomas for years," Dan said. "People still tell me how much they miss my mother even though she passed away several years ago. They were both very involved in the community."

They sat, and after they ordered, Michelle said, "So Dan, maybe we can start by you telling me, in your own words, why you're interested in learning about executive coaching now. Is this something you've always wanted to do?" Then she quickly added, "And by the way, I want you to know our conversation is confidential. I want us to be able to be open with each other."

Dan replied, "That's good to know. As I'm sure you've heard from Will, I'm taking over my dad's position at Richards'. There are a lot of things going on in my life right now that I could use some help with — and not just at work. Will thought you'd be a good person to talk to."

Michelle smiled. "Balance is so important in life, isn't it? So many people think they can compensate at work if their personal life is off and balance their personal life if there are problems at work. When I hear the phrase 'work/life balance' I have to laugh to myself, because it's all just life balance. You can't have one out of whack and expect it not to affect the other. It's all connected."

Dan nodded. What she was saying made a lot of sense.

Michelle continued. "So you said there are aspects of your life you could use some help with. It's important to know that even though we're talking about 'executive' coaching, other aspects of your life might come into play. Like I said, it's all connected. I want the people I work with to be real and honest with me. I want their coaching experience to be meaningful in every way. I believe everyone can have it all in life. When they don't, they just haven't defined what it is they want. They haven't taken the time to examine and understand what's not working or missing, and then create a plan to fix it.

"Coaching isn't a complicated process. You asked how it works. Well, simply put, it means figuring out where you're at and where you want to go. Through coaching, we create a game plan to get you there, and I as your coach help you implement that plan. When you think about it, all professional athletes have a coach. Why would business professionals be any different?"

"I never thought about it like that," Dan said. "To be honest, I guess I've never allowed myself to slow down enough to do this. I've had my foot on the gas as long as I can remember."

"That's good to know about yourself," Michelle said, smiling. "I want to work with people who are absolutely committed to doing the work and who believe they can have it all. I've worked with people who say they're committed, but when it really comes down to doing the work, they aren't. It's a waste of time and money if there's not total dedication and commitment."

As their food arrived, Michelle explained that generally executives want to change or enhance certain aspects of their life to maximize their success and the success of their organization. She handed him a small, glossy laminated card with the word C.H.A.N.G.E. printed on it. She explained it was a mnemonic device she used to help clients understand some of the benefits of coaching.

C.H.A.N.G.E.

Challenge	your current mindset and broaden your awareness
Help	to sort things out and create an action plan for your life
Achieve	your goals through action and accountability
Navigate	through the challenges of a new role that requires additional skills and expertise
Grow	personally and professionally by investing in your life
Energize	your passion and enthusiasm for living

"So how can coaching be beneficial to your new role as a CEO?" Michelle said. "You have the academic knowledge associated with running a business, but you lack the experience. From what you've told me, you're at a critical junction in your career, and having strong leadership and business skills are paramount to your success. Coaching can help you identify and sharpen those skills, particularly when you need to do so without missing a beat."

Dan said seriously, "I have some big shoes to fill, and I'm in over my head. I feel like at any moment I could crash."

"People who don't have a plan are the ones who crash," Michelle replied. "I see it all the time. I think that's one of the reasons so many newly appointed managers and leaders fail. Coaching takes a systematic and proactive approach to change and development. Self-development starts with self-awareness. We start with detailed and in-depth conversations and assessments. I get to know who you are and what you want to achieve. We work together to create a plan around your goals. Then we construct actionable and measurable objectives. Remember, what gets measured gets done.

"One of my many roles as your coach is to hold you accountable for doing what you say you want to do. To use the words of a former client and professional baseball player, 'You're there to give me a pat on the back — or a kick in the pants!' I'm there to help you to get comfortable outside your comfort zone."

"This all sounds good, but what are you thinking in terms of time — thirty days? Sixty?" Dan asked.

"Everyone I coach is unique," Michelle said. "To start with, I don't take on clients without a minimum commitment of at least six months. I wouldn't be doing you a service in a short amount of time. Research shows, and my experience confirms, that to learn new and consistent patterns of behavior or skills takes about five or six months. And it takes another six months for people to start noticing those consistent changes. The time-frame is up to you. It's really no different than learning a new sport. It takes time, commitment, persistence, patience, and discipline."

"Will mentioned he's worked with you off and on for more than two years," Dan said.

"I'm on retainer with several clients. It's not unusual for executives to continue working with me as the need arises," she told him. "As for you, six months is a good amount of time to commit to initially. That being said, at any time for any reason, my clients are free to end their coaching. That's the great thing about it; it's geared completely toward you and your exact needs."

Michelle's confident manner put Dan at ease, and he found himself telling her more about his problems at work, and even a bit about his issues with his sister and his breakup with Julie. The more they talked, the more comfortable he felt.

When lunch was over, Michelle told Dan that by the end of the week she would send him an overview of what they had discussed and a coaching proposal for his review.

They said goodbye, and as Dan got into his car, he saw a text from Will asking to see Dan as soon as he got back to discuss a problem in the sales department.

When Dan got back to his office he saw Will standing outside holding a report in his hand. "I just got these from Carolyn Davis," he said. "It seems there are two people who have been causing some real problems in the sales department for quite a while. Carolyn wanted to fire them months ago, but Mike wouldn't allow it."

As they walked into Dan's office, Will filled him in. "Apparently one of them is spreading some pretty nasty things around about you and your leadership ability to employees and our customers. And the other person is related to you in some way and hasn't made his sales quota for months."

Dan took the report and recognized the names immediately. One was Samantha Sheehan, Abby's best friend from high school, and the other was Keith DeLong, a distant cousin of his. Dan's father had an unwritten policy that he would never fire family or good friends, and people took advantage of it. Apparently he had spoken to both Samantha and Keith in the past about their bad attitudes and poor sales performance, but nothing had changed. Everyone knew Mike would never do anything about it. And now that he was gone, they were out of control. Something had to be done, and fast.

Will said, "You knew sooner or later you were going to have your first defining moment as our new CEO and leader. Looks like that moment has arrived."

"I don't understand what you mean by a defining moment," Dan said.

"Every new leader must prove he or she has what it takes to lead his or her team and organization. In your case, you must clearly define who you are as a leader by demonstrating that you deserve respect and trust. This situation in sales has been festering way too long with no one willing to fix it. This is your defining moment to show this company you've got what it takes to make the tough decisions, see them through, and be a leader. And it starts with making some hard-hitting decisions and doing some house cleaning in sales."

Feeling nervous, Dan said, "I'll take a look at this and talk with Carolyn right away."

He recalled a class in business school in which they discussed the best way to transition employees. The accepted logic was that when possible, out of respect for the individual or individuals, it is best to let them go on a Monday or early in the week rather than the end of the week. That way the person doing the firing has the weekend to think about the decision. As for the employee, they'd have the rest of the week to deal with their new reality and to begin making changes for themselves.

The following Monday morning Dan was prepared and confident that he could handle the situation. He'd had a thorough discussion with Carolyn about Samantha and Keith's attitudes and job performance. When he arrived at work that morning, he asked Carolyn to call him as soon as they arrived. Dan had all the necessary documentation from human resources, and called them into Carolyn's office individually to inform them they were being let go.

Word of what had happened in sales spread through the company like wildfire. It was now crystal clear to the entire company that everyone — including family members and friends — had to perform...or else.

CHAPTER SEVEN

"DAN, HAVE YOU LOST YOUR MIND?!" ABBY screamed over the phone. Dan had just walked in the door when he heard the phone ring. Now he wished he'd let it go to voicemail.

"You have no right to fire Samantha or Keith!" Abby said Samantha had called her, crying and furious, as she left the company parking lot to tell her the news of the terminations. Abby was livid.

"Just a minute, Abby," Dan said. "By any chance did Samantha tell you why she was fired? Did she tell you about the vindictive lies she'd been caught spreading about the company to employees and customers? She and Keith should've been fired a long time ago, but Dad wouldn't do it. And I know for a fact he wanted to fire Samantha but didn't for this very reason — he was afraid of upsetting you. I read everything in Samantha's employee file, and she's been nothing but trouble since she and Brian split. Keith should've been let go years ago, as well. In all the years he'd been with the company, he only made his monthly quota a handful of times. I don't care if Keith is our cousin. That's not a valuable employee."

Abby barely let him finish his sentence before she continued her rant. "You're absolutely crazy to think you can step in and fill Dad's shoes. He and Grandfather worked for decades to build up this company — you can't just turn around and change everything. And what's this I heard about you dating some gold digger from the company's bank? Now that's pathetic! I repeat, Dan: Have you lost your mind?"

That question knocked the wind right out of him. How in the world would Abby know about Liz? He certainly hadn't told anyone. If Abby knew, it meant others at the office might know about it too. And what did she mean about Liz being a gold digger?

"Abby — " he started, but he heard a click and knew she'd hung up on him. He knew people had a tendency to believe in their own perceptions and prejudices above fact. But there were enough rumors circulating about him at the office already. He had deal with this situation as soon as possible. He emailed Will to ask for a breakfast meeting the next day, not mentioning that he wanted to talk about Liz. But Will replied right away — and Dan got the feeling he already knew what the meeting was about.

That night he felt on edge, and even a couple of strong gin and tonics didn't help him relax. His mind kept presenting him with worst-case scenarios as he tossed and turned in bed.

"How is it that I keep taking one step forward and ten steps back?" he thought. It was like his whole life was slipping from his grasp. The clock read 3:34 as he finally drifted off to sleep.

Dan got to the coffee shop the next morning to find Will already there. He'd hardly sat down before Will said, "What the hell were you thinking dating someone from the bank, Dan?"

So he already knew about Liz. "I know this looks bad, but I honestly didn't think it was a big deal," Dan said. "We met each other at the gym about a month or so before Dad died. She told me she worked at the bank. Then I ran into her again shortly after that at Ducey's, and we had a nice conversation. The next day she called me at the office to invite me to lunch. It seemed harmless — and I hadn't dated since Julie left, so…." he trailed off.

"Didn't you stop to think about the possible repercussions of dating someone from our bank — especially someone who works as the assistant to Frank Wilson, the man in charge of the company's loan? If the bank doesn't secure our line of credit — if we don't keep a good relationship going with the bank — we could lose this company."

"But I didn't know who Frank Wilson was when I met her, let alone that Liz worked for him," Dan said in his defense.

Will shook his head and took a sip of his coffee. "It doesn't matter, Dan — what matters is how it looks from the outside. Sales are off, and morale and confidence are as low as I have ever seen. We need that relationship with the bank more than ever. Nothing can jeopardize it."

Dan nodded silently, his face hot. Then Will asked, "And is it true you had something delivered to her at her office? Jude told me this yesterday."

Jude? How did Jude know about any of this?

"Evidently after whatever you sent her was delivered to her office, she wrote about it on Facebook. Several of her coworkers read it and asked her about it. She told them she had hit the jackpot. No more dating losers from the bars. She thinks she's in the big leagues now with you. She has her eye on the prize — you and your money. Well, you can imagine how word spread around the bank over this.

"Apparently it didn't take long before Frank heard about your relationship. He called Jude to ask if he knew that our new company CEO was out fooling around with one of his employees while his company was in danger of failing. Frank doesn't know you, Dan. For all we know, he could be thinking you're dating her to gain confidential information on our status with the bank. Jude relayed this story to me the second he heard it. So what's going on with you?" Will looked angry and, worse, disappointed.

Dan felt like a total fool. He had not considered any of this. "It was just some flowers for her damn birthday. That's all." He couldn't believe such a small gesture had gotten him in so much trouble.

Will put his hand on Dan's arm. "Dan, the only thing any of us can control in life is our reputation," he said. "And whether you meant this to happen or not, you've put yours at risk now with our bank. I'm sure you had no ulterior motive for wanting to date this person, but in most cases perception is reality. Frank is upset over this, and actually, he has a right to be. You have to end it…and now."

Dan couldn't argue. "You're right, Will, and I'm sorry," he said. "I'll take care of it right away." Pushing aside his cold coffee he put a ten-dollar bill on the table and headed back to Richards'.

Once he got to his office, he closed the door and sat in his desk chair staring out the window. How was Liz going to take this? What was he going to say? Should he try to make up an excuse or tell the truth? Dan knew she would be at work by now so he picked up the phone and dialed her direct number.

She picked up immediately, and before he could even say hello she began gushing about how excited she was about their upcoming date and the new outfit she had purchased. When she finally paused to take a breath, Dan said, "That's actually why I'm calling, Liz. I'm sorry, but I can't go out with you again. I didn't realize the repercussions of us seeing each other."

"Repercussions? What repercussions?" she said.

"Somehow word got out that you and I had a few dates, and someone told your boss, Frank. He got upset and called our CFO. He thinks I'm trying to get confidential information from you or something. I'm really sorry, Liz. I like you, but I just can't jeopardize our relationship with your bank."

"Is this a joke?" she snapped. "I'm afraid not," Dan replied. "Unbelievable! Fine!" she yelled, and slammed down the phone. Dan realized she was the second woman to hang up on him that week. He put the phone down and rubbed his forehead with his fingertips.

He felt terrible the rest of the day. The one bright spot was when Carolyn Davis stopped by to tell him she thought morale was already starting to improve with Keith and Samantha gone. Dan was beginning to realize just what it took to run a company like Richards'. His father and grandfather had had more to deal with than he ever realized.

∼

DAN DECIDED TO VISIT GRAMS THAT NIGHT. IT HAD BEEN another rough day, and seeing her always made him feel better. He picked up some fresh flowers from the greenhouse before leaving and drove by his house to pick up Mully, whom Grams loved. When she saw him at the door with the bouquet and Mully, her face lit up. "What a nice surprise!" she exclaimed.

She brought him into the kitchen, and after putting the flowers in a vase and getting some water for Mully, she fixed her eyes on Dan. "What's wrong, Daniel?" she asked.

She'd always been able to see right through him, Dan thought with a rueful smile. So he told her about having to fire Keith and Samantha and incurring Abby's wrath. He also told her a little bit about Liz and how he'd had to end things.

"Grams, what if I made the wrong decision? What if Abby was right, and I'm going to ruin this company? I feel like I can't talk to anyone about this — except for you, of course." Grams gave him a small, concerned smile.

Dan continued. "I can't always go running to Will every time something happens. I need someone to talk to and confide in, to help me get on the right path." His mind went immediately to Michelle Montgomery. He was thankful he had decided to enlist her as his executive coach.

Grams paused for a long moment, then reached over to take his hand. "Darling, I cannot tell you how many times your grandfather felt the same way you're feeling right now. He held most things inside, so when he would open up and talk, I knew things were serious. I would always ask him this: Do you believe in yourself? Do you believe you have what it takes to do what needs to be done? If you don't first believe in yourself, you don't stand a chance. So I'll ask you the same thing, Daniel. Do you believe you can run the company?"

"I honestly don't know," Dan said.

After they chatted for a while, he realized it was getting late, so he collected Mully, said goodbye to Grams, and left. As he drove home, he thought how relieved he was that it was nearly the weekend. He and Vince were going to the lake cabin on Friday, and Dan was looking forward to it. Outside in the fresh air fly-fishing with Vince always rejuvenated him.

When he got home, he got out his grandfather's journal. He turned to the entry marked December 5, 1956, and read:

I have never been much of a religious man. Emily pretty much forces me to go to church with her for Mike's sake. But my church is the outdoors. Working in the garden cen-ter with my hands in the dirt keeps me more grounded and connected with the world more than anything.

Tonight I was cleaning up in the back shop and had the radio on. Everyone had gone home for the day. I heard someone on the radio talking about faith and mustard seeds. I turned up the volume and sat down to listen to what he was saying. I jotted down some notes as I listened, and I hope I can remember all he said. It was quite a mes-sage.

He said that faith is the power of total conviction in the mind, possessing the mind, and cannot be restricted in size.

Belief is even stronger. Belief is knowing. Because you have heard something and been convinced that what you have heard or read is true, you develop a deep belief in what you have heard. You believe it to be true. You believe in a total, complete way that defies contradiction.

He said, "Believe you will receive, and you will receive." Therefore, if you could believe in what you ask for, as powerfully as does a mustard seed know its own identity, you would be able to do anything you want. In other words, the more powerful the feeling and intent, the more powerful the outcome.

There are so many times I think I am not going to make it. I have so much at risk here if this company fails. The man on the radio said, "If you could carry within your mind a seed — the perfected plan of your most sincere goals — and know beyond all doubt that it can grow and come into perfect completion, you would see this wonderful seed take on a life of its own, which would presently manifest in your life."

He ended by saying that if you seek to understand, you will find that little by little, understanding will come to you. Ask. Believe. Receive.

Thank you, Grandfather, Dan said silently. This was exactly what he needed to read tonight.

CHAPTER EIGHT

MICHELLE MONTGOMERY ARRIVED PROMPTLY at Richards' at 8:30 the following Monday. Dan met her in the office lobby and spent some time showing her around the garden center and their newest greenhouse. They then headed back to his office, and as they sat down, Dan said, "So tell me again how this coaching process is going to work."

"Well, that's just exactly what I have planned to talk about with you today," she said with a smile. "First of all, I'm very grateful for this opportunity to work with you, Dan. I want to remind you again that what's discussed between us is strictly confidential. We can't create a relationship built on trust without it."

Dan gave her a nod as she positioned her iPad so he could see the notes on it.

"Let's take a look at how this process works," she said. She explained that her approach consists of four stages, and read each one aloud:

1. **Intake and discovery:** The objective of this stage is to learn all I can about you — how satisfied you are with where you are now, your strengths, and what areas of your life you want to change, enhance, or improve professionally and personally. There are a number of valuable personal and professional assessments you might consider taking. If you agree, I would also like to interview key people in your life to get their perspectives on you.

2. **Goal setting and clarifying expectations:** Approximately 10 percent of people have specific, well-defined goals, and only about 3 percent of those people ever attain them. With my help, you would create your professional and personal goals and your road map for getting there. Your objectives would be quantifiable and measurable. As Michael Phelps one said, "I think goals should never be easy; they should force you to work even if they're uncomfortable at the time." There are no shortcuts in the process of making life changes. Clarity and commitment are essential for success.

3. **Coaching:** We will schedule time weekly to talk either in person or over the phone. Throughout

these conversations, we will be moving forward to convert your goals into realistic outcomes through discussing day-to-day situations and problems. I will hold you accountable for your commitments and help you anticipate and manage any obstacles that might get in your way.

4. **Evaluation:** Together we will create checkpoints along the way to be sure we are both on track and satisfied with the progress being made.

"So where do we start?" Dan asked.

"We start with you," Michelle said, taking out a notebook and a pen. "Tell me about yourself. Start anywhere you'd like."

Dan wanted to get some things off his chest about his dad. "I've always wanted to work here side by side with Dad and show him I had a good business head on my shoulders. But it was like he would never let me in. It's hard to describe. I think he wanted me working here, but there was this barrier or something he kept up around me." He took a deep breath, then looked at Michelle. "This might sound ridiculous, but sometimes I wonder if he even really liked me."

Michelle simply nodded and jotted something down in her notebook. Dan then shifted his focus to business. "We've had a problem with turnover, too. Dad and I constantly butted heads over what to do about it. I've always been a proponent of training and developing the people here. Talent is a leading indicator of whether a business is heading up or down. I told Dad just a couple of months ago, 'No talent, no numbers.' But he couldn't — or wouldn't — believe me when I told him, 'Help them grow, or watch them go.' Dad didn't believe in professional development or training. To him it was a waste of time and resources."

Dan paused for a second. Then he said, "Someday I'd like to know what it was about me that just never clicked with him. I worked hard, I had good ideas, but it was never enough in his eyes. And I have to admit, that's taken a toll on me." Michelle nodded again.

Then Dan somewhat hesitantly mentioned his failed relationship with Julie. She'd said he'd changed since he started working for his father, become more withdrawn and less happy. As time passed, she wanted more of him, and he just couldn't give it.

"So here I am," he said. "I'm in my thirties, single, my self-confidence is in the tank, and my own sister wants to sell this company out from underneath me. I guess you could say I'm in desperate need of some luck."

Michelle closed her notebook. "Well, Dan, it sounds like you're very clear about what's not working in your life. In time, we'll talk about why it's necessary to stop arguing for your limitations. And by the way, I believe luck really has nothing to do with success. But we'll save all that for another time."

She asked him how he thought people perceived him at Richards'. After thinking for a moment he said, "With the exception of Will Butler, no one here knows me well enough to have an opinion. I decided a while back that it was better just to keep a low profile around here."

"Did you prefer it that way?"

"Of course not, but I didn't have a choice while Dad was here, did I? He ran the show. Hell, I was in the top 5 percent of my MBA graduating class. I wanted Dad to know I wasn't an idiot. But what did I get from him working here over these few years? Nothing but ridicule and pushback from him." Dan felt years of pent-up anger boiling up and fought to contain it.

"My first year out of graduate school I told the management team here about a program I had created for increasing profits through social media. Even my professor said it was great. I had worked on it for months. And after I presented it to Dad and the team, Dad actually mocked me in front of everybody. 'You high-tech college boys think you have it all figured out, don't you?' he said. I was totally humiliated.

"And after that meeting when everyone had left, Dad told me, like he always loved to, that neither he nor his father ever had a fancy diploma hanging on their wall. His exact words were: 'So don't you ever think you can come in here and tell me or anyone how to run this company.' So I guess over time — I can't say exactly when it happened — I started to think, 'What's the use?' I lost my fire and my enthusiasm. And it affected my life, and Julie's.

"So you ask me how people perceive me. On the outside, people think I've got it all — the business, prestige, some money. But no one knows what it's really like. I'm disappointed in my stubborn and callous father, my overpowering grandfather, my enabling mother, and my hateful sister, but most of all, I'm disappointed in me. And I want to — no, let me change that — I need to change my life. I need to change my reputation not only here at Richards', but in my family and in the community. Despite what Dad thought of me, I know I have a lot to add to this company." It felt good to get all that off his chest for once.

Michelle said, "You know, there's a quote that says, 'No one can rob a person of their importance except the person himself by his denial of his value.'"

She was right. Dan told her, "In your website you list six questions to ask yourself to see if coaching is right for you. One that jumped out at me was, 'Are there areas of your life you want to improve to bring greater satisfaction and fulfillment?' I think every aspect of my life needs improvement — personal, professional, my health, my confidence…"

He paused. Then he said, "I'm absolutely positive I don't want the same life Dad and Grandfather had. Their personal lives were in shambles. They were never home. Work was their life. I know there's more to life, and I want it. And I am committed to doing what I have to in order to find my answers. "

Michelle smiled. "Then it appears we have some work to do!" she said.

As the meeting wrapped up, Michelle told him she would email him several online personal assessments he would find helpful and insightful. Dan found her calm positivity reassuring, and felt his frustration ebbing a bit. They scheduled another time to talk, and Dan walked her to the elevator. As he waved goodbye, he thought, *Maybe there is a light at the end of this tunnel, after all.*

∼

ON HIS WAY BACK FROM THE ELEVATOR, DAN WALKED PAST Will's office. Will motioned for him to come inside. "How did things go with Michelle?"

"I have a long way to go. And I have a lot of things to fix in my life. It's going to take a lot of work," Dan told him.

Will smiled. "Sometimes to win the game, all you have to do is show up. I remember I felt the same way when I first started working with her, too. But little by little, you'll start chipping away at things and begin to create new mindsets and attitudes. She challenged me and pushed my buttons like no one ever had. But you'll get as much out of this as you put into it. Working with Michelle can change your life — if you're ready for it. Actually, Michelle is the one who first told me about the Five Ps of Leadership. She made me realize that leadership starts with thinking about what kind of life you're leading. You'll see how each one of those will come into play even as you start your coaching with her. It's about defining and planning for what type of life you choose to lead," he said.

Dan was about to say something else when Jude walked in. Will gestured for him to sit down. Jude looked pleased with himself, which Dan didn't take as a good sign. Turning to Dan, Jude said, "I received an interesting call this afternoon. It had to do with your girlfriend at the bank." He emphasized "girlfriend" like it was a curse word. "She's applied for a job here and is using you as a reference!"

Dan was shocked. "What are you talking about?" he demanded.

"It seems that after the shock of you ending things with her wore off, she was furious. Apparently she's one street-smart little gold-digger who saw you as her ticket from living paycheck to paycheck to living the good life. She stormed into Frank Wilson's office and told him, among other things, to bug out of her personal life. And out of respect, I won't repeat the exact words she used with him. Needless to say, she was fired instantly."

"You've got to be kidding," was all Dan could say. And why does Jude know all this? he thought.

"Oh, there's more. She's threatening to sue the bank for wrongful termination. Frank is so upset over this entire thing that you started, he called me to suggest we consider finding a new bank. This has turned into an extremely serious situation. I don't need to remind you what it means if we don't get our credit line extended." His words were angry, but he had a faint, smug smile on his face.

All the positivity Dan felt after his meeting with Michelle had disappeared. This seemingly simple situation had escalated into something quite dire. He wished he'd never gotten involved with Liz in the first place.

He turned to Will. "I had no idea she would react this way. What can I do to fix it? I'll do anything."

Will had already picked up the phone, and as he dialed, he said, "We have to turn this around — now. And we're going to need help. I know just the person. He's the only person I can think of who can help us out of this banking mess. His name is Charlie Rowe."

Then he said to Dan, "And do what you have to do to make things right with Frank."

CHAPTER NINE

JUST WHEN DAN THOUGHT THINGS COULDN'T get any worse, they had. How could he have been so naive? How could he have put his company in such danger without even realizing? *No wonder people don't believe in me*, he thought.

That night after getting home from work, Dan sat in his den with Mully at the foot of his overstuffed leather chair and a fire blazing, lost in thought. For some reason he started to think about Julie. Their relationship started out with such hope and promise. They used to play a silly game they created together called Wishes, Hopes, and Dreams. They would write down everything they wanted to have together on little slips of paper and put them into a big crystal vase in the living room. Julie believed if they wrote their dreams down and believed in them, they would come true. "The universe conspires in every way it can to make dreams come true. You'll see," she would say. Sometime they would tell the other what was going on the slips into the vase, and other times not. That's what made it fun for them.

When they broke up, Dan couldn't bring himself to get rid of the vase, which was half full of little slips of colored paper. He had moved it to a shelf in the guest room so he didn't have to see it every day. But now he walked into the room and pulled out a slip of paper. He unfolded it and read, in Julie's handwriting, "In two years, have a baby and start a family of our own." Loss and regret washed over him, and he sat down heavily on the guest bed.

As he sat there staring at the paper in his hand, his phone buzzed in his pocket. He pulled it out and saw an email from Michelle. It read:

Dan,

To follow up from our meeting today, I'd like to ask you to complete the following survey, and to think about the questions below before our next meeting. When we next meet I'll also have you take the MBTI© survey, which can help identify traits that are intrinsic to your personality.

Survey—Core Values:

Complete the attached document, which will help you to identify what is most important in your life—your core values. In other words, who you are and what you stand for that comes from the core of your being. More specific instructions are at the top of that page when you open the document.

Questions:

Think through the following questions and be ready to discuss your responses when we talk next time:

1. What are your greatest strengths and challenges as a leader?
2. What do you most want to have in your life — personally and professionally?
3. Who are three (business) people you strongly admire?
   a. What is it about them that you most admire?
   b. If they were your advisors, what two or three milestones would you like to accomplish to really impress them?
3. If you had been in your father or grandfather's place, what might you have done better or differently knowing what you know now?
4. On a scale of 1 to 10 (1 = extremely dissatisfied and 10 = extremely satisfied), how would you rate your work/personal life balance? What specific areas do you want to change or improve?
5. On a scale of 1 to 10 (1 = extremely dissatisfied and 10 = extremely satisfied), how satisfied are you with your physical health and overall well-being? What are some specific things you would like to be doing better or differently in this area?

I look forward to our meeting next week.

Michelle

As Dan finished reading the email he was already pondering the questions Michelle had posed. The one that most caught his attention was the one about his father and grandfather. What would he have done differently had he been in either of their places? It wouldn't be an easy thing to answer.

He got up from the bed, intending to fix some dinner, and as he walked toward the door something on the wall caught his eye. It was a framed piece of paper — a poem of some kind, Dan thought. He vaguely remembered seeing it in his grandparents' room when he was a kid, but he came into the guest room so infrequently he'd almost forgotten about it. He stepped closer and read:

"If" by Rudyard Kipling

> *If you can keep your head when all about you*
> *Are losing theirs and blaming it on you;*
> *If you can trust yourself when all men doubt you,*
> *But make allowance for their doubting too;*
> *If you can wait and not be tired by waiting,*
> *Or, being lied about, don't deal in lies,*
> *Or, being hated, don't give way to hating,*
> *And yet don't look too good, nor talk too wise...*

Dan was amazed. He felt like Kipling was speaking directly to him. He read the entire poem twice, but still wanted more detail, so he went into the den and typed "If Rudyard Kipling" into his computer. He learned that Kipling had written the poem for his own son, and it was full of valuable lessons: Follow your instincts and stay positive in the face of differences of opinion and disapproval, but give others a chance to voice their opinions. The easiest resort for a person is to blame his failures on others; it is the basic tendency of all to pacify their ego. One should take responsibility for his actions. Self-confidence and self-respect are the best assets one can own. Nevertheless, self-confidence must not verge on over-confidence and must make room for others' views and beliefs. With patience and perseverance, nothing can stop you.

These were valuable words to remember in trying times, and Dan made a mental commitment to memorize the whole thing. He also decided to take the poem into work the next day and hang it in his office, where he needed it most.

He was tired and getting hungry. This had been one of the first nights in weeks he had an evening to himself. He put on his jacket, grabbed a beer and a steak from the fridge, and headed out to the backyard to fire up the grill. As he was waiting for the steak to cook, he suddenly remembered the envelope Grams had handed him days ago. He reached into his pocket, and pulled it out. On the front of the envelope was written "To Grandfather." He recognized the untidy handwriting as his from when he was a little boy.

He carefully unfolded the faded yellow page and began to read.

Dear Grandfather,

When I grow up I want to be just like you and Dad. And I want to work with my Dad just like he gets to work with you. And then maybe if there is nothing to do, we can go outside and play catch or go fishing.

I will work hard to get smart like you and Dad. I will to go to college because I want to work with you when I get bigger. Then I can help you so that when you come home at night we can play. You will not be so tired.

When I get older I am going to have a son so we can work together too.

When I grow up you and my Dad and I will drive together to the office and see each other all day long.

When I grow up I will be a Super Hero like you. I will be strong just like you and Dad. I will not let you down. I will make you proud of me.

I love you, Grandfather,

Danny

Dan stared at the letter in disbelief. He read again, "I want to be just like you and Dad. I will not let you down. I will make you proud of me."

His steak was done, so he carefully folded the letter and put it back into the envelope. *Where did that little kid go?* he thought. He'd had so many hopes and dreams back then, and no idea of how difficult they could be to achieve. As he ate his steak, he couldn't help wishing just a bit that he could go back to being that little boy again.

∽

THE FOLLOWING DAYS WERE NO BETTER AT THE OFFICE—BUT at least they weren't worse. The bank was still breathing down their throats, and Abby was still hell-bent on selling the company, but it felt like the dam was holding. Something had shifted in Dan the night he read that little letter Grams had given him, and he found himself with renewed drive and determination.

Tuesday morning Will stopped by Dan's office, where Dan was poring over seemingly endless stacks of sales reports and budgets. "Dan, this afternoon I'd like to introduce you to someone I highly regard and who I think can help us through this banking ordeal we're facing. He's not going to be cheap, but I wholeheartedly believe we need him."

"Will, how can we afford to bring in someone — especially after reviewing all this?" Dan said, holding up several of the finance reports.

"If we don't get that bank loan, what does it matter?" Will replied.

He had a point. "This guy can do a lot more for us than you think," Will said. "One thing Mike never realized was the value of bringing in outside help. Yes, we pay their fee, but we don't have to pay any benefits, there are no tax burdens, and we don't have them for life like employees. When you look at what you're paying for and the value they bring, in this situation it makes good business sense. And more important, I've seen what this guy can do. I want you to meet him. He'll be here this afternoon. All I ask is that you meet him and hear what he has to say."

"Sure," Dan replied. "I can use all the help I can get."

That afternoon, Will called Dan into his office. When Dan entered he saw a distinguished-looking man who appeared to be in his sixties sitting in one of the chairs in front of Will's desk.

"Dan, I would like to introduce you to Charlie Rowe," Will said. "If anyone can help us through our situation, it's Charlie.

He's a senior advisor to CEOs of companies all over the nation and has written several books on how to meet the challenges of leadership and management succession."

Charlie shook Dan's hand firmly, and Dan could feel the power and force of a man that has seen it all. He had a no-nonsense look about him, but the twinkle in his eye hinted at a softer nature underneath.

"It's nice to meet you, Dan. Will has told me a lot about you. And I want to tell you how sorry I was to hear about your father. It was a real shocker to hear that he had passed away. I met him some years ago. He seemed like a great guy. He did a lot to build this business."

His voice sounded like one you'd hear on the radio — deep, strong, and commanding. Everything about him exuded intelligence and confidence, and Dan liked him immediately.

"That he did. My dad had a reputation for being somewhat of an SOB, too, and controlled every aspect of this business. I'm sure Will has told you what we're up against with the bank and other things — including my sister, Abby. She wants to get out — to take the money and run."

Will interjected. "Since we last talked, Charlie, I've been closely reviewing the departmental budgets, too. Everyone needs to cut back expenses significantly, but no one wants to budge. Our CFO refuses to cut the budget because he thinks we need to please the bank. Our departments won't cut out anything because they think they're down to bare bones right now, and sales won't budge because no other departments will. This budget situation was starting to heat up right before Mike passed away. I asked him to bring in someone from the outside to help with this, but Mike wouldn't listen. He said he'd solve it all himself."

Charlie said, "You're in a very precarious situation. From what I've heard so far, this company is operating with an extreme silo mentality. In other words, each department is working independently and not in alignment with the others."

Charlie paused a brief moment and looked at Dan. "Before we go any further, I need to know one thing. What do you want to do with this company? You have options. Are you in the same camp as your sister, or do you want to work to bring this back? I can work with you either way. I can repair this banking situation to sell it, and you and your sister walk away with your inheritance. Or we can go the other route — which will be a lot tougher — and fix this mess and turn things around. It's up to you."

Just a few days ago Dan would have been unsure of his answer, but now he replied right away.

"My grandfather started this company with a dream and a loan to buy a piece of land, some equipment, and seeds. He thought that worst case, if his garden center failed, he could at least use the land to grow enough food for his family to survive. He sacrificed almost everything, including time with his family, to make it work. He believed in himself and risked it all to create this.

"In the beginning, his friends and the bank thought he was crazy. Grandfather lived by the saying, 'You reap what you sow.' He believed that with hard work, honest intentions, good people, and unshakable faith and belief, he could make his dream a reality.

"He handed it down to my dad, who, despite his shortcomings, continued to build it to where it is today. Did both men make mistakes along the way? I'm sure they did. Did they have regrets for what they sacrificed to create this? My guess is they did."

Dan took a deep and deliberate breath and said, "I'm sure I'm going to make more mistakes than both of them put together. It appears I'm already off to a flying start." Will and Charlie exchanged a little grin.

"But I haven't had the chance yet to prove myself to anyone here — including you, Will," Dan said, turning to him. "And I'm going to. I want to prove to you, this company, and especially my family that I can successfully carry on this legacy Dad and Grandfather started. I'm not a quitter. But I need help. Lots of it. So, Charlie, you ask if I want to find a way to fix this mess. You're damn right I do!"

Chapter Ten

As a result of their meeting that afternoon, Dan, Will, and Charlie began to chart their course of action. Charlie took the lead on analyzing all the technical and financial aspects of the banking situation. His first action would be to talk with Jude. He also wanted to meet with each of the senior managers to fully understand and analyze whether what they were saying about their budget cuts was accurate.

Dan's responsibility was to restore the relationship with the bank — which he knew was not going to be easy. He scheduled a meeting with Frank Wilson for the following day.

After setting up the bank meeting, his next phone call was to Michelle Montgomery. When he explained his upcoming meeting with the bank, she asked, "What is the purpose of this meeting, Dan? What do you want to accomplish?"

"I want to apologize to him in person. I want to convince him I'm not the person he thinks I am. And I want him to know that I'll do whatever it takes to get things back on track… if it's not too late."

"How are you going to do that?" she asked.

"I'm going to be honest and straightforward. I want him to know I made a mistake and that my intentions with him and the bank are to get past this situation with Liz and move on. He needs to know I am a man of my word," Dan said.

As a result of their brief talk, he felt more self-confident and clear-headed. He realized how valuable it was for him to have someone to listen while he talked through things. He thanked her for her time, and as he hung up the phone he realized the most remarkable part. Michelle gave him no advice. She merely asked the right questions for him to find his own answers…and his own voice.

∼

AS DAN ENTERED THE BANK THE NEXT MORNING TO MEET WITH Frank Wilson, he felt like every single employee was giving him the evil eye. How many of them knew about Liz and him? Before he could dwell on it too much, Frank's assistant, a woman in her fifties named Ruth, gave him a cup of coffee and a kind smile and showed him into Frank's office.

The office was a marvel of organization. Frank's desk and back credenza were as neat as a pin. Every stack of paper was in perfect alignment, and Dan noticed a pen on the desk placed exactly parallel to the well-organized files. The thick glass that covered the top of the exotic burlwood desktop was spotless. Frank was seated behind the desk and did not stand as Dan entered. "Hello, Dan," he said. "Have a seat, and let's get right to it." Dan had barely managed to sit down in one of the wooden-backed chairs in front of the desk before Frank said, "I need to know where Richards' is in specific relation to the information and projections I requested last week — Tuesday to be exact — from Jude." He folded his hands on the desk and looked expectantly at Dan.

Dan took a breath. He knew it was important to say the right thing to avoid making a bad situation any worse. "First of all, Mr. Wilson, thank you for agreeing to postpone our meeting for a few days. I don't mean to delay any further, but there's something I need to say before we get started. And that's this: I'm sorry. I'm sorry for the problems I created for you and for the bank through my brief relationship with Liz. I offer no excuses other than to say that I didn't consider the short- and long-term repercussions of dating one of your employees. I actually didn't even know she was your assistant until recently.

"I didn't think about what possible problems it could have created from your perspective. Liz could have been privy to confidential information about our loan — and you would have no way of knowing whether confidential information had been disclosed. I assure you that nothing like that even came close to happening, but I know it damaged my already sorry reputation with you." Frank looked surprised but said nothing. Hopeful, Dan continued.

"This bank has had a long relationship with my company. My dad and the previous bank president, Steve Giles, worked together over several decades, and I'm sure Mr. Giles had his share of ups and downs with Dad, too. But Comstock National has always hung in there with our company. I'm only now beginning to appreciate the importance of what Dad did by building and maintaining his relationship with this bank. I only wish he would have included me or a few others in it."

Frank still hadn't cut him off, so Dan pressed on. "But that's water under the bridge. What's important now is how to go forward…and I hope we can go forward working together. I intend to continue to build the relationship my dad worked decades to create. You don't know me from Adam, and I haven't given you a very good impression of myself starting out — but I give you my word that I am committed to doing whatever it takes to repair and sustain a good working relationship with you and ensure the future of my family's company."

There was a pause. Finally Frank spoke. "You're absolutely correct when you say I don't know you," he said. "I've worked with companies all over the area, and in recent years I've seen ones I thought were rock-solid fail completely. The problem I continue to see with businesses today is management. As much as 83 percent of loan failure over the past ten years has been traced back not to cash flow, but to poor management. And that's what really concerns me about you, Dan — your leadership. What is your plan for managing this company and pulling it through this potential crisis you're in? I have yet to see any plans you have in place. I haven't seen any strategic plans or any of the other documents I asked for over a week ago. Not one thing."

Stunned, Dan asked, "What do you mean you haven't seen anything? Jude told me days ago that he was going to send over everything we've put together on the inventory management program you requested, as well as our monthly financials. You received nothing?"

"Of course not! Why do you think I'm so unnerved? I haven't received one thing I asked for from your company."

Dan tried to hide the fact that he was livid. "Well, you have every right to think this way, Mr. Wilson. I take full responsibility for this and give you my word that by the end of business today you will hear from me regarding all this."

As soon as Dan left Frank's office he called Will. "Tell Jude to clear his schedule for the rest of the day, and meet me in his office in 20 minutes," he said. "I want to know exactly what the hell is going on here."

Will was already in Jude's office when Dan got there. Jude was sitting at his desk, and Dan leaned over the edge and glared at him. "Start talking," he said.

"Don't get all hot and bothered about all this, Dan. I told you I was going to get him the documentation, and I will. I didn't know you had this meeting scheduled. Don't try to put all this on me!"

Dan could feel his blood starting to boil. Will jumped in. "Okay. Okay. Jude, what do you have ready to give the bank? And where are you with all the other reports they requested?"

"I would've had everything completed two days ago, but all my time has been eaten up by that idiot running around here... Charlie, or whatever his name is. He's been harassing me, asking a million ridiculous questions about superficial things that don't concern him and that I don't have answers for. I think it's absolutely ludicrous he's even here!"

"Are you saying you don't have anything ready for the bank?" Will asked.

"No, I don't. And I'm not just going to put lipstick on a pig and send some reports to them just to give them something to read. I need time. And I want that moron to get out of my department and let me run things the way I did when Mike was here."

"That 'moron' happens to be a lifelong friend of mine, Jude," Will snapped. "That 'moron' has more business expertise, knowledge, and common sense in his little finger than most people can ever hope to have in a lifetime. He's here to help us in every way he knows how to understand and get us through this situation we're in. And every one of us here, me included, is going to do whatever it takes to assist him — or just get out of his way and let him do what needs to be done."

There was an uncomfortable pause as Jude stared sullenly at the floor and Will tried to calm down. Then Dan said, "Here's what needs to happen, Jude. You're going to get these inventory management program reports done today. What do you need to make that happen?"

Jude looked outraged and began to splutter protests. "I can't possibly get that completed today! It'll take hours, and I promised my son I'd pick him up early from school —"

Dan cut him off. For the first time he felt clear-headed and confident in what needed to be done. "Pull everyone necessary from your team to get that inventory report completed. I want it on my desk by 4:30 — no excuses. And you better call your wife to tell her you'll be working late for the next couple of days. These other reports need to be completed in the next two days, and before anything is handed to me, I want it reviewed by Charlie Rowe. That's his name, by the way: Charlie Rowe. I want him to sign off on everything before it comes to me. Do I make myself clear?"

The anger had faded from Will's expression as Dan spoke, and now he looked astonished — and proud. Jude, on the other hand, was scowling. But Dan didn't care. "Do I make myself clear?" he repeated. "I don't want to see 'lipstick on a pig,' either. I want every report done to absolute perfection and clarity."

"Yeah, yeah. So get out of here and let me get to work." Jude was fuming.

Will and Dan walked out together, and as they walked down the hall, Will turned to him and said, "Where did that come from?"

Dan was still fired up from the conversation. "The other day Michelle emailed me this exercise to help me clarify and understand what's most important to me in my life. She called them my core values. One of the values that surfaced for me was courage. I guess it came forward just now in that meeting, huh? And maybe one of those 5 Ps came through, too: purpose with determination."

Will smiled. "I guess it did," he said, and slapped Dan on the back.

As they turned the corner they saw Charlie coming down the hallway. "Just the two people I need to see. Do you have some time to talk?" he asked.

They went into Dan's office, and Charlie closed the door. "Something just doesn't make sense to me," he began. "I've spent that past few days poring over your financial statements, and things aren't adding up the way they should. There seems to be pockets of missing information. I tried to get some answers from Jude, but he stonewalled me. He became more and more defensive with each question I asked, so I decided to give up with him for the time being. I was getting nowhere fast."

Charlie continued. "Then I met with several of your senior managers to get a better understanding of their thoughts on the budgets and forecasts for the coming year. Everyone seems to be all over the place, with no clear direction on justifying spending. There doesn't seem to be any cohesiveness whatsoever between any of the departments. I believe everyone gets along well, but when it comes to their departments, they're hoarding anything they can get. The thought process is more, 'What's best for me and my department?' rather than, 'What's best for the company?' Clearly, departmental silos exist here, and they need to be dismantled if we're going to make this company work."

Dan filled Charlie in on the conversation he and Will had just had with Jude, and warned him to be ready for the possibility of some anger and passive aggression directed his way.

Then Will said, "Charlie, I didn't tell you this because I didn't think it was important at the time, but I think it's important now. Mike hired Jude basically out of obligation. Jude is the nephew of his wife, Rita. He was laid off from his former job and couldn't find work after months of interviews and rejections. He went to Rita and begged her to ask Mike to hire him — and Mike could never say no to Rita.

"I always thought Jude had a feeling of entitlement when it came to this company; that he should be next in line to take over. Especially since Mike kept Dan, his own son, on a tight leash and for some reason wouldn't allow him to progress in management and leadership.

"When Rita passed away, I approached Mike about finding a new CFO. It wasn't that Jude was doing a bad job, but there was so much more he could've been doing to help the success of this company. But Mike wouldn't hear of it.

"I have no concrete evidence of this, but I think Jude eventually just began to assume he would take over. Mike never mentioned anything to me, but Jude started to act cockier and cockier around the office, ordering people around above and beyond what his job responsibilities required.

"Then when Mike died, Jude immediately came to me to ask what plans had been put into place to fill his position. I told him Mike had no formal succession plans other than those stipulated in the will, which named Dan and Abby as the rightful heirs to the company. He asked me to check again, and of course I told him the same thing. Since Abby had no desire to be involved with the company and Dan was already working here, it became obvious that Dan was the likely person to fill Mike's position. And now I think Jude was even more put out by that than he let on."

This was the first Dan had heard of any of this. But if it was true, it explained a lot. Thinking back, Jude hadn't looked very happy when Dan showed up at Richards' the day his dad announced he'd be working there. And Dan seemed to mysteriously get left off a lot of emails detailing important meetings. Dan was starting to wonder just who had been putting thoughts into his dad's head about his job performance. Could Jude have been undermining him this whole time?

CHAPTER ELEVEN

AFTER CHARLIE AND WILL LEFT HIS OFFICE, Dan checked his calendar and realized Michelle would be there in less than an hour. He was looking forward to discussing the results of the surveys he had taken. He remembered taking the Myers-Briggs Type Indicator© in graduate school, but couldn't recall his results.

He was finishing typing an email when Michelle tapped on the door to his office.

"May I come in?"

"Absolutely, Michelle. Nice to see you. Have a seat."

As she sat, she took several large files out of her briefcase and put them on his desk. "We have lots of things to discuss today, and it should prove interesting for you. This isn't as much coaching today as it is explaining — I feel it's important that I make that distinction."

"Great," he said. "I'm eager to see the results."

"How about if we start with the MBTI© survey?" she asked. "I use this survey with all my coaching clients because it gets to the core of who you are — the innate aspects of your personality. Of all the personality assessments out there, I think this is one of the best because it's easy to understand and can give so much valuable information about you. Another reason I use it is because there are no right or wrong answers with your results. It simply reports what you prefer in terms of the four dichotomies, or polar opposites, of the MBTI© framework. I think you're going to find this valuable."

Michelle gave Dan a brief overview of the history of the MBTI© and how it describes one's preferences. She explained that just as people have a hand they prefer to write with, they can still use both hands — it's just that one feels more natural. The same was true with MBTI© preferences. Michelle said that as she explained each of the four aspects of the MBTI©, one of the two preferences would more than likely stand out to Dan because it seemed more natural to him.

Then she handed Dan a pocket-size laminated card that read:

MBTI© 4-Part Framework

Energy	**E**	**Extraversion** Talk things out	**I**	**Introversion** Think things through
Gather Information	**S**	**Sensing** Attention to details	**N**	**Intuition** Attention to big picture
Make Decisions	**T**	**Thinking** Logical implications	**F**	**Feeling** Impact on people
Lifestyle	**J**	**Judging** Joy of closure	**P**	**Perceiving** Joy of processing

MBTI is a registered trademark of Consulting Psychologist Press, Palo Alto, CA

Michelle began to explain the first dichotomy of energy and how people prefer to get energized. Essentially people gather energy by being either more outgoing and talkative (extraverted) or more reserved and quiet (introverted). Dan told her that while he liked quiet time occasionally, it helped him to talk out the things that were on his mind, so he skewed more naturally toward extraversion.

Next she described how people prefer to gather information. Dan said he studied details that were necessary to know (sensing), but for the most part he preferred to have the big picture and generalities (intuition). Michelle said intuition was akin to having a sixth sense. "That reminds me of when I would read industry reports in grad school and would get these gut feelings sometimes that Dad should try some of them," Dan said. Michelle smiled. "That was your intuition coming through," she told him. "It seems to be a very clear aspect of your personality."

The third aspect of the MBTI© represented decision-making preferences. Michelle explained that some people prefer to consider the logical implications of the decision first; in other words, they first apply a more impersonal and logical analysis as they make decisions (thinking). Those who prefer the opposite preference, feeling, first consider the impact on others in decision-making and then apply logic. This preference was a coin toss for Dan. He closely considered how decisions would impact people like his family and his employees first — but that type of reasoning was closely followed by considering the logical implications of that decision. So while it was close, Dan decided he leaned more toward the feeling side.

For the last dichotomy, Michelle asked Dan, "Are you the type of person who enjoys the journey or getting to the destination?"

It was an interesting question, Dan thought, and easy for him to answer. "I enjoy getting to where I'm going."

Michelle then described the last aspect of the MBTI© framework: preferred lifestyle. She explained that people with a driving sense of urgency to get things done and checked off their list are more prone to a judging preference. Dan had always been an avid list-maker and always had a desire to complete things once they were given to him — even when he was a child. Michelle said that was his judging preference in action. Perceiving, the opposite of judging, meant people were more spontaneous and energized by doing things at the last minute and going with the flow. That didn't fit Dan at all.

As they finished up the questionnaire, Dan said, "So according to this, my MBTI© preferences are ENFJ. So that means I prefer to talk things over with someone else — extraversion —

as I'm hashing through things on my mind. I prefer to have the big picture and generalities of a situation and details only as needed, which is intuition. When it comes to making big decisions, I first consider how people will be affected and then closely consider the logical implications, which means I pick feeling as my first preference, then go to the logical implications. And lastly, I'm a consummate list-maker and I rarely wait to the last minute to do anything — a joy of closure/judging type."

"Exactly, Dan," Michelle said, smiling. "Your personality preferences are part of who you are, just like your eye color or being right-handed. If you were to take this survey again 15 years from now, your results would probably be the same. It's who you are."

Dan nodded. Michelle continued, "It doesn't really matter who you are in terms of your MBTI© preferences. It's great information to know about yourself, but what really matters is what you do with it. This is information that can impact every aspect of your life and that you can benefit from for the rest of your life. In terms of business, this framework can be used for resolving conflicts, planning strategies, marketing, influencing and motivating others, making sales, managing people… the list goes on and on. This information can be a life saver in your personal life, too, but for the sake of time we'll just stick to business right now.

"Think about your strengths and weaknesses as they relate to your personality preferences. As you build your executive team, you will want to consider surrounding yourself with people who complement your preferences; in other words, people who are not the same as you and who can provide that balance. For example, you're more of a big-picture strategic thinker — an intuitive, or N type — and prefer details as needed. You will want some people on your team who are more naturally attentive to details — sensing, or S, types — because that isn't necessarily a strength for you. See where I'm going with this?"

"Yeah, I do," Dan said, rubbing his chin.

"So many people get into leadership roles without knowing themselves through a framework like this, and it honestly is one of the common reasons they fail. The MBTI© can give you a lifetime of information about yourself and about understanding others. It's not just something you learn about today and put on the shelf. The more you really learn and understand this framework, the more you will find you can't live without it. It will help you speed-read every person you come in contact with. That's pretty powerful, if you ask me!"

Dan found the idea fascinating but still wasn't quite sure how he could use it to help him at Richards'. As if reading his mind, Michelle asked, "So how might this relate to business and your leadership style?"

"I'm not sure yet," Dan confessed.

"You now know you're the type of person who prefers to think out loud and to talk through things that are on your mind. But what if you're working with someone who prefers to think things through first and is more quiet and reserved — introverted — like your office manager, Georgia? Or what if you're working with someone who's more concerned with understanding every single fact and sorting through each little detail?"

"Frank Wilson is like that. He lives for details," Dan said.

"So what if you're going through your daily conversations and interactions with people oblivious of the differences? That's where communication can break down," Michelle pointed out. "Many of us are on autopilot when it comes to interactions with others. We assume everyone communicates the same way we do. But as you can see through this simple framework, people are different and can have completely different styles when it comes to communicating, gathering information, decision-making, and the way they go about their daily lives.

"Among other things, I think the MBTI© is an excellent frame-work through which to listen to and understand others. It's an outstanding tool for understanding both yourself and those around you. So when you're talking with someone like Frank, who is saying things like, 'Tell me exactly how this is going to work,' or, 'Who specifically is going to do this?' you can tell this person is in a sensing or detail-oriented mode. And what do you do? You 'flex' — meaning you adjust your response accordingly. You answer precisely and with the appropriate amount of detail, even though your style prefers the big picture and generalities. It's that simple, and that difficult."

"Why do you say difficult? It seems pretty straightforward to me," Dan said.

"Like I said earlier, Dan, most people are on autopilot when it comes to communicating. Without thinking, we tend to respond in our preferred style and don't take the time to listen to the type of language someone is using. I always say, 'It's not what you say as much as how you say it.'

"To be an effective leader, it's essential to have excellent communication skills. You've got to have a built-in radar when it comes to knowing and understanding people and learning to speak their 'type' of language. By using this framework, you can actually determine people's type as you talk with them. It works with email, too.

"When Katharine Briggs and her daughter Isabel Briggs Myers created the MBTI©, they wanted to enable individuals to grow through an understanding and appreciation of individual differences in healthy personalities and to enhance harmony and productivity in diverse groups. They wanted it to be used for, among other things, the constructive use of differences. So instead of letting differences we might have with another get in our way, we can use this as a framework for listening. It will point you in the right direction for changing your approach with that person, if necessary, through the type of words you use. You can flex to another simply through the words you use. Learn to recognize and use the other person's preferred type of language, not your own."

Then Michelle gave Dan his first coaching assignment. It was to list at least ten people he worked with daily and to try to type them. Then she asked him to consider how he might flex his style to be more effective when interacting with them.

This should be interesting, Dan thought.

He was feeling thirsty, so he excused himself and went to the kitchen to grab a couple of Perriers. When he got back to his office he handed one to Michelle, who thanked him. He sat down and took a sip as she brought up his core value questionnaire.

"What did you think about doing that exercise? What did you learn about yourself by doing it?" she asked.

Dan considered his answers. "It was difficult for me to narrow all those possible values down to only four or five," he said. "Courage I identified first, followed closely by family. Family includes not only my immediate family, but also my friends, the people here and our customers.

"Achievement was next. I'm not afraid of hard work and trying new things. If I give someone my word that I'll do something, I do it. It's not an ego thing, either. I simply want to do the best I possibly can by the time I promise to do it."

He then thought about what life at Richards' had been like when Mike was at the helm. "Working here with Dad — well, I've already told you about that. I wanted to do more and have more responsibility and authority, but he wouldn't give it to me. It almost felt liberating to acknowledge that I deeply value achievement and conviction. I want to do more for this company. I just hope it's not too late." He paused, swallowing back emotion. Michelle waited quietly for him to finish.

"And the last core value is authenticity. I want to be the kind of person people can depend on to be genuine and real. If I make a mistake — and I've made a few lately — I own up to them. And I want people around me who are like that, too. Will and Charlie Rowe are great examples of people who are the real deal. There's nothing phony or superficial about either of those men. I value that immensely."

Michelle nodded. "Tell me what you valued about your father," she said, leaning forward.

"I valued his determination and work ethic. But to be quite honest, there were a hell of a lot of things I didn't value. Although our employees were fiercely loyal to him, I didn't agree with his use of fear and intimidation. He micromanaged everyone. He wasn't a teacher or a mentor. He did everything himself. On the rare occasions Dad delegated a task to someone, he watched them like a hawk. Almost always he'd take over and do it himself. No one ever did things to his satisfaction. And he could have one hell of a temper.

"He was also opposed to trying new things. And this company wouldn't be in the position it's in now had he included more people in what was going on and the decisions he was making. He should've included Will in his relationships with the bank, our suppliers, and vendors. He didn't. He only told Will things on a need-to-know basis. That's not leadership, as far as I'm concerned."

Michelle listened intently. When Dan finished speaking, she closed her notebook and sat back in her chair. "There are a couple of other things I'd like you to do before we meet next time, in addition to the assignment I gave you. How would you feel about keeping a journal?"

Dan had to smile a bit when she mentioned it, thinking of his grandfather. "I'm open to it," he replied.

"Great. The first thing I'd like you to write about is the type of leader you aspire to be. Write about who your heroes are and why. Start writing down everything that comes into your mind about leadership, business, your goals, relationships, et cetera.

"Second, I want you to buy a book called *Lessons in Leadership and Life: Secrets of Eleven Wise Men*. Charlie Rowe is a very unassuming man, but he wrote this book, and it is excellent. I think you'll enjoy reading it — and getting to know him better."

Dan was a bit surprised. Will had not mentioned Charlie's book to him, and Dan found himself eager to start reading it.

As Michelle put her folders back into her briefcase she asked, "So what did you find of most value today from all this?"

"I found your explanation of the MBTI© interesting — particularly how it relates to business," Dan said. "We learned a little about it in graduate school, but your explanation was great because you tied it to business and its practical applications. I'm eager to learn more about how to use it here."

As Michelle left his office, Dan checked his watch and realized it was 4 o'clock. He decided to check in with Jude on the bank reports he'd requested. Charlie was seated at the small conference table in the corner of Jude's office reading when Dan knocked on Jude's office door.

"How are things going in here?"

"I don't know. Why don't you ask him?" Jude said peevishly, jerking a thumb in Charlie's direction.

The comment didn't seem to faze Charlie in the least. He looked up at Dan and said, "Everything seems to be in order. I think this is on target for what the bank is looking for right now."

Dan asked Jude, "How soon can I expect to see the other documents?"

"Everyone is working overtime now. I'll let Will know when they're ready."

"You will let me know, Jude. Will has a full plate working on everything else. I want you to go through me."

Jude sighed audibly. "Fine," he said.

Dan sensed Jude's resentment and decided not to let the attitude slide by.

"Look, we're all under the gun here and are working hard and long hours. What's up with you?" he asked.

"Nothing, okay? I just want to get past all this and have it all over with."

"Is there anything you'd like to get off your chest?" Dan's instincts told him there was more to the situation than Jude was admitting.

"No!" Jude snapped. "I have a lot to get done in a very short window of time, so please just let me do my job." He bent his head and pretended to be reading studiously, though it mostly seemed like he was avoiding eye contact.

"Okay, well, have the rest of those reports to me ASAP," Dan said. Charlie handed him the stack of documents that were ready, and Dan headed to his car, intending to follow through on his promise to Frank Wilson and drop them off at the bank. After he'd done so and was about a mile from the bank, his cell phone rang. "Dan, it's Charlie. I know this is short notice, but how about meeting me for dinner tonight if you're free? It's been a long day, and — "

"Of course I can meet you, Charlie," Dan interrupted. "Great idea."

"Perfect. Asia Bistro in half an hour?" Charlie said.

"See you there," said Dan.

CHAPTER TWELVE

CHARLIE AND DAN ARRIVED AT THE RESTAU-
rant at the same time and were seated in a booth in the back
of the small restaurant. Charlie ordered a glass of Merlot for
each of them, and when they arrived he raised his with a smile.
"Cheers," he said. Dan tapped Charlie's glass with his. "Cheers,"
he repeated. He'd been hoping for an opportunity to get to
know Charlie better, and he was glad Charlie had suggested
dinner.

After they ordered, Charlie said, "Dan, I know we haven't
known each other long, but I already have a lot of respect for
you, which is why I have some things I'd like to tell you. I've
listened to you describe your problems, and I think I can help
you figure out how to start to dig yourself out. You've been pro-
tected from reality for too long. Let's see if you can get beyond

your concerns about your ability to survive what you think is a crisis."

He reached into his lapel pocked and pulled out a small, folded piece of paper, which he handed it to Dan. "This was given to me many years ago, and since then I have shared this with people like you. Here. Read it."

Dan took the paper and began to read.

The longer I live, the more I realize the impact of attitude on life. Attitude, to me, is more important than facts. It is more important than the past, than education, than money, than circumstance, than failures, than success, than what other people think, say, or do. It is more important than appearance, gifts, or skill. It will make or break a company. A church. A home.

The remarkable thing is that we have a choice every day regarding the attitude we embrace for that day. We cannot change our past; we cannot change the fact that people will act in a certain way. We cannot change the inevitable. The only thing we can do is play the one string we have, and that is our attitude.

I am convinced that life is 10 percent what happens to us and 90 percent how we react to it. We and we alone are in charge or our attitudes.

It was signed "Charles Swindoll."

As he read, Dan recalled Will's lecture about the importance of attitude the first day he took over as CEO. Come to think of it, Michelle had told him the same thing — that attitude at the beginning of any task will determine its successful outcome.

He finished reading and looked up at Charlie. "This is some powerful stuff," he said, stretching his arm out to hand the paper back.

"Keep it. It's yours," Charlie said with a little smile. "I gave this same quote to another young man several years ago, too. He was a lot like you, Dan. His name was Ken Wilson. His situation was different from yours, but he, too, had his demons to slay."

Dan re-read the paper as Charlie took a patient sip of wine. Then Charlie said, "I don't think it's a coincidence that behind every great man or woman you'll find a teacher or mentor whose knowledge, experience, and wisdom have been passed on with a positive impact.

"My dad was my first mentor, and I depended on him for advice. My family went through tremendous ups and downs when I was young. But we were committed to staying together and working through our challenges. The most powerful force in human affairs is the realizable wish."

Dan was mesmerized. Charlie had managed to not only survive the challenges thrown at him, but to thrive because of them. Somehow he had developed the ability to navigate through rough waters and come out better as a result.

Feeling a bit foolish, he said, "You must think I'm pretty pathetic — to have had all these advantages and to still feel angry and resentful."

"Not at all. You have to realize that you're being tested by life, as we all are. I had a lot of mentors along the way who made me feel good about myself. You should only listen to that kind of person. Ignore the critical comments by others."

"But how do you stay positive when things get tough?" Dan asked.

"When I was young, I was very close with my grandmother, as Will tells me you are. She was a big influence in my life. She told me that the mind is its own place and in itself could make a heaven of hell and a hell of heaven. I had to take control of my mind. Whenever I felt sorry for myself I would think of my grandmother's advice," Charlie said.

"But so many things feel out of my control," Dan said. "As soon as I almost have a handle on one problem, three more crop up."

"Again, it is all about attitude and perseverance. Remember, the sword is best sharpened by that which it cannot cut. You're going through the sharpening process," Charlie replied. "And don't feel like you're alone in this. Will is a fantastic business-man and can be a very important mentor for you. He was always a big help to your father. Will cares for you like family. And I was happy to hear you're working with Michelle Mont-gomery — she's one smart lady."

That jolted Dan's memory. "She recommended I read your book, *Lessons in Leadership and Life*."

Charlie looked a bit surprised, but seemed pleased. "It's a story of how I helped someone much like you to get his life back. His name was Ken, the young guy I referred to earlier. I've been blessed to have known some amazingly brilliant and success-ful people who mentored and taught me along the way. Their stories helped Ken, and I thought capturing them in book form would let me help many other young people like him."

"I'm looking forward to reading it," Dan said sincerely.

Charlie smiled again. Then he said seriously, "One of the most important things you should do now as a leader is to find some mentors for yourself. Will most certainly is one, but you should have more than that. In my book, I wrote about eleven of them I've known and their secrets to success.

"Mentors are there for you to share their experiences — both successes and failures. They model professional behavior and teach what can't be taught in school. They're there to advise you on complex situations that may not have a single right answer or approach, and to offer observations and explanations that can help you learn. Mentors support and offer reassurance when learning becomes difficult or overwhelming."

The waitress had come up to the table with their check, and Charlie grabbed it before Dan could. "I'll get this one," he said. "You can get the next!"

"Thanks, Charlie — for everything," Dan said. "You've given me a lot to think about."

Charlie nodded. "There's nothing in life you cannot be, do, or have as long as you believe in yourself and keep good supporting people around you to help. Remember that." Charlie stood to put on his coat. "You're a good man with a lot of potential and…" he trailed off, one arm still out of its sleeve, his head turned toward the door. "Do you see what I see?" he said softly.

Dan turned to look and noticed two men heading toward the foyer of the restaurant. From their spot in the back of the restaurant, Dan got a clear look at their faces. One of the men was his cousin Jude. And the other was Grant Evans — the president of their biggest competitor, Bridger Landscaping.

Dan was astonished. He was ninety percent sure Jude and Grant didn't know each other socially — and there was no business reason he could think of for them to look so friendly with each other.

"I think I smell a rat," Charlie muttered.

They waited to leave the restaurant until they were sure Jude and Grant were gone. As they walked to their cars, they decided the first thing on the next morning's agenda would be to discuss what they'd seen with Will.

~

DAN GOT TO THE OFFICE VERY EARLY THE NEXT MORNING AND noticed that Charlie and Will's cars were already there. He could see the light on in Will's office and headed that direction. The building was empty and quiet, and Dan could hear Will's voice all the way down the hallway as he approached his office.

"He was what?" Will demanded. "And with whom?"

"Good timing," Charlie said as Dan walked in. "I was just getting to the really interesting part."

"You mean seeing Jude with Grant Evans isn't interesting enough?" Will shouted.

"Yes, there's more."

That was news to Dan. He pulled a chair up to the desk and sat, while Charlie remained standing.

"When we left the restaurant last evening I wasn't in the mood to go straight home, and I decided to stop by the club for a quick nightcap. As luck would have it, several of my golfing buddies were still there just finishing dinner. Grant Evans is a member there, too, and I asked them whether they had ever seen him with Jude. One of the guys said he had. He recalled seeing them together the week after Mike's funeral. He thought it was unusual, but just chalked it up to coincidence. I asked them to just keep this between us but to give me a call if any of them ever saw the two together again."

Will opened his mouth to speak, but then in walked Jude with several folders Dan assumed contained the reports he'd asked for the day before.

Quickly assuming a nonchalant expression, Will said, "So, did you burn the midnight oil last night?"

Jude, looking even more rumpled than usual, said, " Well, somebody has to." He tossed the folders on Will's desk and left.

"That was close," Dan said.

"No kidding," Will said. "Let's keep a very close eye on Jude and this situation. We still need him until we have this bank problem put to bed. We'll confront the situation when we have more information. For all we know it could just have been a friendly dinner together, however unlikely that situation is. Do you both agree that we proceed with extreme caution?"

They agreed that given the present situation, that was their best bet. Charlie then asked Dan if he had time for some updates on several action items.

"I have time right now," Dan said.

When they were back in Dan's office, Charlie began, "I know you have a lot on your mind right now, especially with what we saw last night, but we need to shift gears. You know I have met with four of your department heads regarding their financials, budgets, and strategic plans, and everyone's all over the place. I don't mean to put this on your father, but as far as I can tell, this company has really never had a vision or a roadmap for the future. These people don't know how to be part of the strategic planning for this company. Mike did it all and never included the management team.

"What you need around here is more collaboration and a sense of community. And that starts with you, Dan. I think you need to get out there and talk with the people who work here. Listen to them. Hear their stories. Get to know them, and let them get to know you a bit more. Until you know people personally, how can you lead them professionally?

"Business is about relationships. You're already learning that with the brief interactions you've had with Frank Wilson at the bank."

Dan wholeheartedly agreed. It was time to get to know the people who worked for Richards' — really get to know them — and, more important, for them to get to know him.

After Charlie left, Dan decided to take a few quick minutes for himself. He had stored his grandfather's journal in the side drawer of his desk, wanting it to be available for him to read as time allowed. Now he took it out and opened it to a page Grandfather had written in the spring of 1957. The company was ten years old, and his father was nine.

I believe things are starting to come together. I don't know what I would have done without these people working here. The newspaper yesterday had this quote: '*No duty is more urgent than that of returning thanks.*' It got me thinking. I have entire families working here now — husbands and wives, and even some of their children. I'm not often one to do this sort of thing, but I wanted to tell the people here how much I appreciate their loyalty and hard work.

So after lunch today I wrote this on a sheet of paper and hung it on the wall of the coat room:

> *I know I don't say this too much around here, but I want every one of you to know how much I appreciate all your hard work.*
> *But don't think this means you can have a raise.*
> *Gabe*

Josephine and Mary Savage are two sisters who have worked here since I started. They came to me tonight as I was leaving with tears in their eyes after reading what I wrote. "No one says thank you anymore," was all they said, and each gave me a hug.

After reading that, Dan called Georgia the office manager and asked if there were any relatives of either Josephine or Mary Savage still working at Richards'. To his surprise, she told him two of Josephine's grandchildren were, and were currently in the garden center. Dan grabbed his jacket and headed out to find them.

Chapter Thirteen

"It was an amazing conversation," Dan told Michelle that afternoon when they met for their coaching appointment. "John and Eldon Savage have been working here for several years—they're twins, just a couple of years younger than me, and I told them I'd read about their grandmother from something Grandfather had written and would like to buy them a cup of coffee. The three of us talked for almost an hour, and I got to thank them and their family for the amazing loyalty they've shown us through the years."

John and Eldon had told Dan their grandmother had worked at Richards' for twenty-six years, their parents had retired recently, and they had both started about seven years ago in delivery.

"It made me realize I'm part of something bigger than me and that all of us — all the employees, my family, their families — are in this together. So many negative things have happened lately, and I've just been trying to hold on. It was good to do something for someone else for a change; to change my focus from me to others — if only to say thank you."

Michelle smiled at him. "That reminds me of a quote by Buckminster Fuller: 'You can rest assured that if you devote your time and attention to the highest advantage of others, the universe will support you, always in the nick of time.'" It all boils down to this — leadership and life are about relationships. If you think about the definition of a relationship, it is the way in which two or more concepts, objects, or people are connected or relate to one another.

"The true nature of our relationships, whether personal or business, is to learn about ourselves through our interactions or relationships. Care more about what you think of yourself and who you are than about what others think. That way you stay authentic, ethical, honest, and true to yourself and, therefore, to others.

"The conversation you had with John and Eldon uplifted them, and that uplifted you. You cannot give something to another without also giving it to yourself. Everything has consequences. And ultimately is boils down to this: People just want to know that you care and that they matter. The two basic needs all human beings have are to be noticed and to be heard. It's as simple as that."

Dan knew exactly what she meant. Michelle continued. "But now we should get back to you! If you had to say one thing, right now, what is it you would say that you ultimately want in your life?"

Dan thought for a few seconds. Then he said, "I want to find my voice again."

"Okay, good," she responded. "So what does 'finding your voice' look like to you? If you found your voice, what would your life be like? How might it be different? How might your life change?"

Those were questions he'd never asked himself, and he needed time to think about them, which he told Michelle.

"That's perfectly understandable," she told him. "You've mentioned you're enjoying writing in that new journal. How about if you add that topic to your journal to-do list? And while you're at it, I'd like you to write about success. For example, what comes to mind when you think about success? How does trust fit into the equation? How would you define success — professionally and personally? What can you do now to be more successful? How does this relate to trust? What are leadership traits and characteristics you value? What are the keys to success and building trust?"

"Hey, too fast!" Dan interrupted. "How am I going to remember all this?"

Michelle laughed. "Don't worry — I'll put all this in an email to you when I get back to the office."

"Phew," Dan joked. "On a different note, I noticed on your website that you have a special niche for working with salespeople, is that right?

"I sure do. I started this business years ago working specifically with and coaching sales people. Why do you ask?"

"Our sales manager, Carolyn Davis, could use some help. I believe we have one of the best sales teams around, but they need help. Could you give her a call when you have some time and talk with her?"

"Absolutely. I'd love to," Michelle said, glancing at her watch. "Oh, my gosh, I have to get going! I'll be in touch!" She confirmed their appointment for the following week and dashed out.

Later that afternoon, Michelle emailed Dan the journaling suggestions from their meeting. She also mentioned that since Dan had so much success meeting with John and Eldon it might be beneficial to continue meeting with other people in the company in the same way. Then she asked him if he had started going back to the gym. Dan had identified that as one of his goals, and had told her last week he was going to start going again that week.

The truth was he hadn't made it there yet. He thought of the refrain Michelle had taught him: "Do it right. Do it now. Do it right now." He picked up the phone and called his old personal trainer to arrange an appointment for that weekend. Then he called two of the four supervisors Charlie had met with and arranged individual meetings with them for later that day.

~

THE NEXT AFTERNOON DAN MET WITH THE FOUR SUPERVISORS and realized Charlie's observations were correct—the company lacked vision, planning, and communication. People had respected his father, but clearly Mike had held all the cards. It wasn't that they lacked motivation—they didn't understand what was expected of them.

So before leaving for the day, Dan sent an email to Will and Charlie. He was thinking of one of the 5 Ps of Leadership — planning — as he wrote the subject line:

Strategic Planning and Offsite Meeting

Will and Charlie,

It's becoming more apparent that to go forward we need to step back and do some planning. This company needs a new mission that defines what we are doing. We need to redefine our values and what we all stand for as an organization. Our managers need help to create strategies that zero in their key approaches to success and to write goals and action plans — weekly, monthly, quarterly, and yearly.

Time is of the essence. I've asked Georgia to check with you and our department managers to find the first available time we all can meet offsite and get working on this. I know this is short notice, but we need to get the wheels turning.

Any additional specific thoughts or ideas, as well as potential obstacles you might foresee, are appreciated.

Dan

He got home that night to find an email from Charlie with a CC to Will.

Dan:

Excellent plan to begin building your strategic frame-work. It's nice to see you are putting that MBA to work! If you don't have a roadmap for where you are going, how can you be upset when you don't get there? A company's success depends on how well you define and live by this framework—which includes your mission, vision, values, strategies, and goals.

This type of cooperative planning can work miracles in terms of dismantling your departmental silo mentality, as well. In addition to continuing your work with the bank, this is your most important initiative now...for you and for the leadership of this company.

It's like Gertrude Stein says: "It's awfully important to know what is and what is not your business." That is so true personally and professionally. So until our meeting, I advise you to be thinking about your business—what is and what is not your business. The vision statement could coincide with the goals of your father and grandfather. The vision should state what you ultimately intend this company to be in the future, in terms of growth, values, employees, contributions to society, and so on.

Only half of all small and family-owned businesses actually have a written strategic plan, and even less have a written succession plan. I have years of experience working with this sort of thing. Please let me know how I can help.

Charlie

That got Dan thinking. He went to his computer and opened the file within his MBA folder called "Richards' Business Plan." Part of his coursework had been to write an entire business plan. It had taken him the whole semester to create it, and it contained everything from a proposed mission and vision statement to goals and specific action plans. Dan had received the highest grade in the class from his professor. Elated, he had emailed the plan to his father and was eager to get Mike's feedback on it. He still remembered, word for word, the short email his father had sent back. "Your grandfather didn't need any complicated business plans, and I certainly don't either. I have things perfectly under control here, and there's no need for any of this."

Dan just shook his head as he remembered how he had felt after reading his father's response all those years ago. And then he said out loud to himself, "Sorry, Dad, but things have changed."

He spent the next three hours with Mully at his side re-reading the entire plan and updating it to account for new technology that was now available. It was still pretty solid, he thought to himself. He then emailed it to Will and Charlie with a short note explaining what it was.

Almost immediately another email popped up in his inbox. But it wasn't from Will or Charlie. It was from Jude.

I hear you're planning a little company meeting offsite and not including me. To use your words from the other day, Dan, start talking.

Chapter Fourteen

Strangely enough, as Dan arrived at the office the next morning there was a message on his desk the office manager, Georgia, must have taken the night before after he left. It was from Abby. All it said was "Call me ASAP." He got a sick feeling in the pit of his stomach.

But then he remembered Michelle's words from their coaching meeting the other day about relationships: "Their purpose is to learn about ourselves through interactions with others." What was it about his relationship with Abby that he needed to learn about himself?

I can think of a few things she needs to learn about herself! he thought.

Abby had many great qualities, but there were things about her that had always rubbed him the wrong way. She was overly competitive and self-centered. She was judgmental and quick to form opinions, and once those opinions were formed, there was no changing her. And lately she had this sneaky way of communicating with him. She would call when she knew he wasn't around or when she had no time to talk and hear what he had to say. Dan added "manipulative" to the mental list.

So how best to deal with her now? Recalling the core value exercise he'd done with Michelle, Dan opened the file in his computer and looked at the list again: courage, family, achievement, and authenticity. He thought about how to apply those in this situation as he dialed Abby's number.

"Hi, Abby, it's Dan. I'm returning your call from yesterday."

She sounded impatient as she said, "I don't have a lot of time to talk right now. I'm getting the kids ready for school, and..."

"Here's the deal," Dan said, cutting her off. "This call is important and I want you to sit down for two minutes and listen." She stayed silent, so he kept going. He could hear the kids in the background.

He said as calmly as he could, "I'm getting tired of the games you're playing lately, and they need to stop. You and I have been given a tremendous responsibility with this business. I know you want to sell it. You've got no ties to it, but I do. Every day since Dad died, I've been learning and appreciating more about what he and Grandfather sacrificed for this company, and I'm not going to let it go.

"Family matters to me, Abby. But this business matters to me, too. You matter. I want to include you in what's going on here and not fight with you." He paused, waiting for her response. He heard her sigh loudly, and braced himself for some harsh words. Instead, he heard a click and then silence. She had hung up on him — again.

"Well, isn't that interesting?" he said as he put the phone back down. Surprisingly, he felt very good about that phone call. He had stayed level-headed, honest, and clear about his intentions. He had clearly defined his purpose with determination.

He looked at his watch and realized he was almost late for the meeting in the conference room Will had called regarding the bank. He was the last to arrive. "Sorry I'm a bit late," he said as he entered. "I had to make a quick phone call." Will, Charlie, and Jude were already there looking through papers.

"Not a problem," Will said. Dan sat down next to him across the table from Charlie and Jude. "We're making good progress now. Dan, whatever you said to Frank at your meeting has helped. He doesn't seem quite as panicked. But that doesn't mean we can sit back and assume things are going to be fine. There's still a lot that needs to be done. Jude, where are you with finalizing those working capital reports?"

"I've hit another roadblock," Jude said, tugging at his tie. "Those outside offices are totally worthless. They're not getting me their numbers, so I have nothing done yet. I'll call Frank and tell him we need some more time."

"That's unacceptable, Jude," Will said. "First of all, you are no longer to have contact with anyone from the bank without permission from Dan or me. Second, if you need to get into your car and drive to those locations today to physically get those reports, I expect you to do it. But you shouldn't have to. You're the CFO, for Pete's sake."

"Exactly!" Jude cried. "I am the CFO, and that's why I should be talking to the bank, not someone who's never been in a bank meeting before last week." He shot Dan a quick angry glance.

"Like it or not, Jude, I'm head of this company now, and this is how we're going to do things," Dan said as calmly as he could.

"Well, like it or not, you've been screwing up everything lately," Jude shouted, pointing a shaking finger at Dan. "You're going to undo everything Mike worked his entire life to build. You have no idea what you're doing, and you're going to fail and take us all with you. You have no business running this company, and everyone knows it."

Well, there it was. Jude had finally said exactly what he thought to Dan's face, and in front of Will and Charlie. There was a moment of quiet as everyone in the room considered Jude's outburst, then Will opened his mouth to say something, but Dan held up a hand for him to stop. It was time for him to handle this himself.

"It must feel good to get that off your chest," he said to Jude, making sure to maintain eye contact with him. "My guess is that you've been holding that in for quite some time." Jude just sat there with his arms crossed, a scowl on his face.

"Let me tell you this," Dan continued. "I decided that you were to have no further communication with the bank. And here's another thing. This company is going to be successful with or without you. At this point, the decision is all yours. What's it going to be? Where's your allegiance?"

Jude was so taken aback by not only what Dan had said but also how calmly and confidently he'd said it that he was momentarily speechless.

Taking advantage of the silence, Dan turned to Charlie and Will. "Gentlemen, is there anything either of you would like to add?"

Will was first to speak. "You've been part of this company for years, Jude. But things have changed. Things have to change in order for us to make it through this. All of us, myself included, were kept in the dark over most things when Mike ran this place. And we're all experiencing the repercussions of that antiquated leadership style. We have a lot of catching up to do and changes to make. But Dan is running the show now. He's our president and CEO. Hell, he's the owner of this company now. And he needs all of our help."

Charlie stepped in next. "I'm an outsider here, but I've seen this before when there are unexpected changes in leadership at the top. It's a big adjustment for everyone. I'm a straight shooter and call things as I see them. I honestly believe you have a potential star player with Dan. He's young and lacks the experience you and Will have, but I believe he's got what it takes. And he knows he can't do it alone. He has his ego in check — I think he's asked for help at least five times just since I've been here. He needs your help, too, Jude. It's like Dan just asked — are you part of this team?"

Charlie looked at Dan when he was finished talking. "So, Jude, are you in?" Dan asked.

Finally, Jude spoke. "This is bullshit. It's obvious you're ganging up on me. To say I am to have no more contact with the bank is ridiculous. You don't own the company — Abby has equal share. Don't forget that. And why was I not asked to attend your offsite planning meeting? You say I'm needed, but why was I not included? Mike would never have done that."

Dan was quick to reply to him. "Georgia told you about the offsite, I'm guessing. Right?"

Jude nodded.

"What she failed to tell you is that there are more people to be included. I'll speak with her about sharing information that's not hers to give out. But of course you're to be included on matters like this. Next time, though, I ask that you forgo the snide emails and talk to me directly about things. Okay?"

Jude gave a small shrug of acknowledgment.

Will spoke next, "So what can we realistically expect in terms of getting this last report ready for the bank, Jude? What do you need from Charlie or me to help you?"

Jude stood up. "Nothing. I need nothing," he said, sounding defeated. "I'll have all the necessary information pulled together by the end of the day. If there's nothing more, I'll excuse myself." Dan nodded, and he turned and left the conference room.

"I didn't see that coming," Will said. "Dan, I commend you for not getting rattled over that. I was ready to jump across the table and grab him by the throat!"

Dan shook his head. "Emotions like that have no place in business. They serve no purpose other than to add fuel to the fire. Jude said I have no idea what I'm doing and that I have no business running this company. That may be the way he sees things, but it's not the way I see it anymore. This company has needed new life breathed into it for years, and we now have the opportunity to do it. Jude is entitled to his opinion. And I'm sure there are others who think the same way. But it's exactly as I said: This company is going to be successful with or without them."

The rest of the week continued with relatively few shock-waves. They had a meeting on Friday with the bank to prepare for, and all available hands were diligently refining and final-izing reports and documents. Securing that line of credit at the bank was what determined whether Richards' could stay in business.

In the back of his mind Dan had hoped he would have at least gotten an email from Abby after their phone call, but it seemed she and her attorney were off of the radar for the time being. He reasoned that it gave him time to focus and to stay on track with the bank.

That afternoon as he pored over spreadsheets, reports, and documents, Dan was reminded of a few key facts he'd learned in business school. The statistics on family-owned businesses report that they make up more than 80 percent of all busi-ness enterprises in North America and account for 60 per-cent of wages paid and 78 percent of new jobs created. The gap between the employment and job creation figures report family-owned businesses as one of the fastest-growing sectors of the economy. Their new job requirements outpace current employment rates when compared with other businesses.

But Dan also knew that family-owned businesses face some of the most difficult challenges and hurdles. Topping the list was the tricky issue of generational transition. The failure to successfully transition to the second and third generations was largely attributed to either the heirs' lack of interest in running the business or their failure to make drastic changes while at the helm.

So what about when the business is unexpectedly thrown into your lap with no mentoring, no leadership training, no discussion or communication about anything, and no succession plan? Dan thought. Where's the data on that? No wonder the bank was unnerved — *he* was unnerved.

Still, he was determined to do all he could, mentally, physically, and emotionally, to make things work.

The day of the bank meeting came way too fast, but Charlie assured him they had everything the bank had requested and then some. Will, Charlie, Jude, and Dan had triple-checked their numbers, reports, and documents and were confident they had all the information they needed.

Charlie, Will, and Dan decided to drive together to the meeting. Jude told them he would meet them there. The meeting went well, but Dan sensed something was wrong. Frank Wilson went over the documents with them, discussing each individually, and although they had an answer ready for every question he asked, he remained unimpressed and a bit stand-offish. Dan couldn't figure out what the problem was, and he exchanged a few puzzled looks with Will and Charlie throughout the meeting.

As the discussion wrapped up, Charlie said, "Frank, you've been awfully quiet in this meeting. Is there something wrong or that we're missing here? Will, Dan, and Jude have done everything you've asked for and then some. I personally made sure of it. You seem pretty distant, and I'm curious to know how you stand with everything we've presented to you so far."

Frank's eyes darted toward Jude, then fixed back on Charlie. "I apologize," he said in a measured tone. "You have indeed presented all that has been asked for. I need to review all this in more detail and then present it to the Credit and Loan Committee. I should be able to tell you more within the next three weeks."

"Three weeks?" Charlie started, but Dan put a hand on his arm, not wanting to jeopardize the shaky peace they'd made. "Thanks, Frank," he said. "We'll look forward to it."

After the meeting Jude immediately headed to his son's soccer game. Will, Charlie, and Dan walked in silence to the car. Once they were all inside, Charlie exploded.

"This is crazy! Three weeks? This doesn't make any sense," he exclaimed. "There's no reason he couldn't have just given us a verbal okay in that meeting. All the numbers are good; everything is squeaky clean. I know this bank. I've worked with them for years, and something like this doesn't have to take that long to pass through any committees! Something is wrong — very wrong — and by God, I'm going to find out what it is."

CHAPTER FIFTEEN

As Dan rounded the curve into the company parking lot Monday morning he noticed Michelle's car in one of the visitor parking spaces. He momentarily panicked, thinking he might have forgotten a coaching appointment with her. But then he recalled Carolyn Davis telling him that she and Michelle had been in contact regarding the sales team and that they might schedule a meeting. He decided to stop by the sales department before going to his office to say hello and take a peek at the meeting.

But Carolyn's office and many of the desks in the sales department were empty. Then Dan heard voices coming from the large conference room down the hall. He walked toward it. The door was open, and inside was the entire sales team, both standing and seated around the table. Carolyn and Michelle were at the front of the room. From the sound of things, Carolyn had just finished introducing Michelle to the group, and Michelle was in the process of sharing more of her background with the team.

"Before I started my business, I was in sales and sales management myself — so I know firsthand what it's like to be in your shoes. I recently read some facts about sales from the US Bureau of Labor Statistics that might surprise you: One out of every nine American workers works in sales! Each day more than 15 million of you earn your keep by trying to convince someone else to buy something. The United States has more salespeople than factory workers. Did you know the American sales force outnumbers the entire federal workforce by more than five to one? If every single one of you out there selling were to live in a single state, that state would be the fifth largest in the country. So you can see, you're not in this alone!"

Michelle could tell she had the group's attention. She continued. "Selling has come a long way from the old ABC approach — 'Always Be Closing.' In other words, get the order, collect your money, and move on. I'm not saying that isn't important, but I am saying that selling takes more today. Customers are more educated and savvy than ever before. With the click of the mouse they can access almost anything they need to know about what they think they need. But what they think they need may not always be right. That's why they need you.

"A new approach and mindset is vital to connecting with today's population of informed consumers. They usually already know about the features, advantages, and benefits of what they want to buy before they even talk with you. What customers are looking for from sales professionals today is a partnership focused on making the best decision for them. A partnership must be built on honesty, fairness, and clarity. Let me tell about a new model that enhances the old ABC approach. It has more to do with your style and how you present yourself, your services, and your company. This approach is called ACT: attitude, clarity, and trust.

"You know that actions speak louder than words. Your attitude should convey a belief in yourself and in what you have to offer first and foremost. Your communication must be clear and honest. It's vital to get clarity about your customers' specific wants and needs. And with a positive can-do attitude and clarity, you do what you say you're going to do. You build trust."

Michelle paused as she looked around the room. Then she said, "Carolyn tells me the morale around here has been low these days. Would someone like to explain why they think that is?"

Eric Johnson, one of the salespeople sitting in the middle of the room, was first to speak up. "How are we supposed to stay motivated when everywhere we look it's doom and gloom?"

Someone sitting next to Eric, whom Dan couldn't quite see, added, "Yeah, we turn on the television or the radio and everything is negative. We hear it from our customers all the time. How do we keep positive attitudes with all that?"

"What's the magic bullet for staying upbeat?" someone shouted from the back of the room, where Dan was standing.

"These are all good questions," Michelle said. "Sounds like you're looking for some words about motivation and attitude, is that right?" There were nods and murmurs of agreement. "And you think there's a magic bullet?"

"You know what she means," someone else chimed in. Dan was impressed with the energy in the room, and was glad he'd showed up in time to listen in.

"Well, to begin, let's talk about your thinking. Did you know there is right thinking and wrong thinking?" Michelle asked. That question quieted the group. "What are some ways you activate wrong thinking when it comes to what you do? In other words, what thoughts might you be thinking during the day that could be sabotaging your success?"

"You mean things like 'I can't do this, what's the use, there's no business out there, I've tried this or that and nothing is working'?" asked Sandy Bone, who was sitting toward the front.

"Yes! Excellent." Michelle said. "You get where I'm going with this. What are other 'wrong thinking' thoughts you've had?"

"I have a good one," someone said. "Our longtime customers have either gone out of business or have drastically cut back on their spending."

Another almost interrupted to say, "I'm afraid I won't have a job tomorrow because things are so bad."

"So let me ask you this," Michelle said. "What is your purpose for being here — at work — besides bringing home a paycheck?"

There was a noticeable pause. Finally one young lady, in the back of the conference room near Dan, said, "I'm here because I really like what I do and I believe I'm making a difference. Some of my best friends are working here, too. When it comes to making a living, it's just as important for me to make a difference as it is to make a dollar." Some of the group nodded their heads in agreement.

Another said, "I'm not afraid to say this—I like making money! I like the thrill of bidding those big jobs and winning. It's the thrill of the hunt." Nodding accompanied that statement, too.

"Well, it sounds like while there are some real challenges you're facing, most of you enjoy working here and being here," Michelle said. "So let me ask each one of you sitting here right now—what is your mind set? Is it set on success, or is it set on failure?

"You asked whether there's a magic bullet. I'll tell you my secret to maintaining a positive attitude, staying motivated, and achieving success. It's this: mindset. It's kind of like selecting a station on your car radio. Are you tuned into positive thoughts and feelings of success, achievement, fulfillment, and enjoyment? Or is your internal 'radio' tuned to the stations of failure, doubt, and fear?

"Remember the saying, 'You reap what you sow'? In other words, what you broadcast comes back to you. Don't forget that that pertains to your thoughts and feelings, too, and not just your words and actions! What you think about and give your attention to is what you bring to your reality. Your thoughts are as powerful as your words and actions. You cannot harvest apples from thorn trees or wheat from weeds. You can't expect good things to come from bad. Think about this and understand this example, because it's very important—not only today, but throughout the months and years to come. Your thoughts, feelings, words, and actions create your future circumstances. Whatever you broadcast with your thoughts and feelings are exactly what you will get back. As the say goes, we reap according to what we sow. There are no exceptions.

"If you want to change your lives and experience success and abundance, tune into those thoughts. Change your words coming from those thoughts. Change your actions arising from those thoughts. What's in your mind will create all your experiences — your unhappiness, frustration, or fear, or your future success, happiness, and fulfillment."

Michelle walked to the other side of the room to address different audience members. "Let me give you another example. Let's say a colleague or customer asks you to do something for them. Remember that you reap what you sow. Now think about what you would like him or her to do for you if you also had that need. How would you like to be responded to?"

Carolyn Davis, who was standing next to the wall in the center of the room, said, "I'd want that person to help me out, too."

"Right," Michelle said. "But there's more to it than just that. It's not only what you do that counts — it's *how* you do it. Think about your reason and motivation. If you help someone only for personal gain down the road, what will you reap in the future? What have you put into motion by doing something for another for your personal gain or benefit?"

A young man in his early twenties raised his hand and said shyly, "So you're saying if I do something from the standpoint of pure selfishness, greed, or ego, or just for my personal gain, then what I could get back is more negativity and problems? But if I give from the mindset of sincere helping and friendship, I could reap some good stuff back someday? So in other words, what I think, say, and feel about something is exactly what I'll eventually get back."

Michelle smiled. "Exactly. Your future circumstances are totally up to you. In all situations — at work, in our communities, in our families — we need to work together in a spirit of cooperation. Remember that people may forget your words, but they will never forget how you made them feel. It's all part of building trust.

"If you want to create success, happiness, a rewarding career, whatever it is — sincerely think it, feel it, talk about it, draw pictures of it, tell stories about it. Let it consume your thoughts and consciousness.

"If the news is bringing you down, don't watch it. There are many other ways of staying up to speed on what's going on other than inundating yourself with television news.

"So if you are anxious about your tomorrows, you're making your tomorrows burdensome and tired even before you get to them! If you tune in to worry, you get more things to worry about. You reap what you sow. Why do it? What good does it do? When did anxiety ever accomplish anything for you? Worrying is using your imagination to create something you don't want.

"Look forward to what's coming because you can't go forward looking at what is or looking back. Think about what you want to accomplish and begin to 'pre-pave' your intentions. In other words, get out in front of what you want to accomplish with your positive intentions before they happen. Look forward to what you want to be, do, or have.

"Don't dwell on the things you don't have or the parts of your life that aren't working perfectly. Remember that what we think and talk about is what we will get. Think about the things that can be yours, and turn your internal radio dial to encouraging thoughts. Give all your attention to deliberately allowing it to come to you, and believe without fear of contradiction. Think more thoughts that are rich with power and certainty, comfort and ease, eagerness and clarity, passion and success.

"As another saying goes, 'You can't put new wine in old containers.' If your mind is full of thoughts that aren't serving you, do some housecleaning and get rid of them — permanently. And don't wait. For most of you, what I'm suggesting is a new way of thinking. I can see it from the looks on your faces! I invite each one of you here in this room to re-imagine how you've been thinking.

"More important, listen to what you're telling yourself. Become aware of what thoughts might be circulating between your ears that could be sabotaging your desired success. Are your thoughts secretly derailing your positive intentions? What kind of life are you planning and forming in your mind? Is your mindset one of competition or collaboration? Is your mindset one of lack and limitation, or of abundance and success?

"As I began this talk, I told you about ACT: attitude, clarity, and trust in selling. And I asked you to think about what kind of sales job you're giving yourself through becoming more aware of the thoughts and messages you're giving yourself. I hope you can see it's your attitude and belief in yourself that determines what you can be, do and have in life. Get clear about what you want, and trust that those positive results are coming. Simply put, the kind of life you will experience begins in your mind. Your life is fashioned by your deepest and most strongly held beliefs and by those ideas and opinions in which you have the strongest faith.

"I asked you to think about what you're thinking. A good question to constantly ask yourself is this: Are you directing your thoughts, or are your thoughts directing you? Exercise mind-full thinking. Think your thoughts deliberately and with positive intention. Don't be sloppy in your thinking."

Michelle paused for a moment, then added, "It really boils down to this: By indulging in your thoughts of fears of what might happen, you're creating the very conditions you want to rectify.

"Whatever you profoundly believe yourself to be, good or bad, success or failure, you will become. Whatever is sent out from your mind and heart returns to you in due course in some form or another. Remember that like attracts like. Strong emotional thoughts are 'consciousness seeds' planted within your orbit of consciousness. These will grow, bearing a like harvest for your reaping."

She looked at Eric Johnson sitting in the middle of the room again who had asked the original question about how to stay motivated. "So you asked how you're supposed to stay motivated when everywhere you look it's doom and gloom? Direct your mind and your thinking with clear and positive intentions — and trust that those changes are coming. ACT!"

"That's all? Why didn't you just say that to begin with?" Eric joked.

The conference room erupted into chuckles. "Thanks for the tip!" Michelle responded and pretended to write herself a note.

Then she said, "One of my mentors shared this with me, and I'll share it with you. Success and abundance expand proportionally to match desires. The fastest way to get to the success you want is to look at the pleasing and positive things you already have. For in the seeking and finding of that which is working, more success and accomplishment will come, and it will come quickly. Your success is the result of your consistent thoughts and feelings of success. Rid yourself of your thoughts of resistance, because as you can now see, resistance will only bring more of the same. Instead, feel appreciation and eagerness for what is coming. None of us can rely on outside sources for answers and help. It's up to us individually and collectively to make that change."

Dan sensed a mood shift in the room from Michelle's words. They recognized the value in her suggestions.

"One last thing," Michelle told the group. "An idea without a goal is just a dream. What gets measured gets done. Set realistic and sensible goals for yourself. Help each other.

"Do whatever it takes to create goodness, and goodness is yours. Do whatever it takes to create success from the standpoint of positive intention, and success is yours. It's time to examine where your mind is set and what you're allowing to fill your thoughts. After all, you can't escape your own mind — you carry it with you wherever you go."

After she finished speaking, the sales staff clapped loudly, and Dan noticed many smiling faces. It seemed they needed to hear Michelle's positive message as much as Dan had.

People had begun to file up to Michelle to ask questions. Dan started toward the front of the room to say hello, but then his phone buzzed. He looked at it and saw a text from Will: "Come to my office ASAP — Charlie has urgent news." Dan gave Carolyn and Michelle a quick wave goodbye and a thumbs up and headed for Will's office.

CHAPTER SIXTEEN

DAN WALKED INTO WILL'S OFFICE TO FIND Charlie pacing around the office while Will sat at his desk looking worried. As Dan closed the door, Charlie said, "I wouldn't have believed this had I not heard it with my own ears. The more I thought about that meeting at the bank, the more I began to realize that things were just not adding up. Something wasn't right. So I decided to do some snooping around. Last night I think I stumbled onto something. Something big. Brace yourselves, gentlemen."

"What in the world is it?" Dan asked at the same time Will said, "What is going on?"

Charlie took a long, deep breath and shook his head. "I've been in business for a long time, and over the years I've created and maintained some stellar relationships with some top-notch individuals. Anyway, last night I had dinner at the club with my golfing buddies again, and, as usual in this day and age, they were commiserating about things. They all know I'm doing some work for you. One of my friends said, 'Well at least Richards' has an out through all this.' I asked him what he was talking about. He told me Bridger Landscaping is planning to buy Richards' — and that Jude is going to be the next CEO."

Dan felt like he'd been sucker-punched. "What?" he managed to say.

"This can't be true!" Will exclaimed.

"I assure you it is," Charlie said grimly. "My friend was even a little surprised I didn't know it. He assumed we had already talked to the bank."

He finally sat, and continued. "Here's the story according to my dear and trusted friend. After Mike's unexpected death, Jude honestly believed that you would never have the guts to step up to the plate and take over for your dad as president and CEO. And that even if you did, you would fail miserably and have to sell. So Jude made it his business to find a buyer that would be ready to step in the second the bank refused to extend your credit line. Jude's arrangement with this new buyer included making him the new CEO.

"Dan, Jude has been working behind the scenes for months — or longer, for all we know — with Bridger to arrange the sale of this company for his personal and financial gain. And Jude has been feeding your sister false information since your dad's funeral, it seems. I believe this has been driven by jealousy and a false sense of entitlement."

Will and Dan both stared at Charlie. Not wanting to believe his own cousin was capable of such duplicity, Dan asked, "Are you absolutely sure this is accurate and truthful information, Charlie?"

"If this is true, the consequences are dire for Jude," Will added.

"I haven't yet seen any physical documentation or proof regarding this," Charlie said. "Nor have I spoken directly to Jude. All I have is what was told to me by an extremely trusted friend. So you ask if this is truthful information, Dan. I believe it is more truth than fiction. Is it a coincidence we saw Jude and Grant at dinner together? Is it a coincidence my friends have seen them together?"

Will rubbed his forehead with his fingertips. "We agreed after we saw Jude and Grant together at dinner that night that we would cautiously continue going forward until we got evidence regarding Jude," he said. "Well, I'd say we have started to get it. We need to confront Jude for his side of this story immediately. We have everything hanging in the balance now with our banking situation, and Jude could tip everything in the wrong direction."

"I agree," Charlie said. "We need to think strategically and tactically on how best to handle this."

Dan's mind whirled, but one step was clear to him. "I want to be the one who confronts Jude," he said. "He was hired by my dad out of obligation to my mother. He's my cousin, and I am the president of this company. I want to be the one to look him straight in the eye and ask him for the truth — about everything. I'm sick to my stomach that this could be happening, but as I was reminded not too long ago, nothing escapes consequences. If Jude has done any of this, he must own up to the consequences of his actions. It's time he and I have a man-to-man conversation and let the chips fall as they may."

Charlie and Will nodded. Dan added, "And another side note to all of this. This company is going to have clear and defined plans and structures in place for dealing with nepotism and favoritism. That is going to be a major topic at our upcoming offsite meeting."

"Excellent idea," Will said.

"Can you give me until this afternoon to confront Jude?" Dan asked Charlie and Will. "I need some time to think about all this and plan out exactly what I want to say and how to proceed. I need to mentally prepare myself for what I might hear."

Will said, "That should be fine — just be sure to get this taken care of by the end of the day. I'll keep my eye on him and make sure he stays in the office until the end of business today. And I'll check with our legal counsel, Phil Oberrecht, about how to handle this. You do what you need to do, Dan, and I will cover things here."

Dan thanked Will and Charlie for their advice, then went back to his office and shut the door. On the wall next to his desk he had hung his grandfather's framed copy of Kipling's "If" that he had brought from home. He read part of the second stanza:

> *If you can bear to hear the truth you've spoken*
> *Twisted by knaves to make a trap for fools,*
> *Or watch the things you gave your life to broken,*
> *And stoop and build 'em up with worn-out tools...*

Dan recalled that his grandfather had actually written about this specific stanza somewhere in one of his journals. He got out the volume he had been reading and flipped through the pages until he found the entry he'd been thinking of. It was like Grandfather was sitting there talking to him through the pages.

May 21, 1961

The business has tripled in size since I started it 14 years ago, and I've had more than my share of ups and downs — and surprises. And I've made mistakes along the way. But as Kipling says, "Play through the lies/losses/mistakes silently; maintain dignity in the face of possible defeat. And if one witnesses the devastation of things he's built, and rebuilds the same with a rekindled fire, nothing can stop him."

These words by Kipling help me through the tough periods to "hold on when there is nothing in you except the will which says to them: 'Hold on.'" I have to be stronger than anything life and this business can throw at me.

I am the leader of this company, and responsible for my actions as leader. I believe Napoleon Hill said it best: "Success requires no explanation. Failure permits no alibis."

Dan sat at his desk for a long while, lost in thought about his grandfather's words. He knew he had to maintain his dignity, but the more he thought about what Jude had been doing, the angrier he got. He needed someone to talk to about this, someone objective. Then he remembered Michelle. He picked up the phone and dialed her number, and was relieved when she answered.

"Michelle, I know this is really short notice, but do you have a few minutes to talk?"

"Of course, Dan," she said, sounding her usual warm, upbeat self. He briefly explained the details of the situation, struggling at points to keep the anger out of his voice. "So how are you going to handle this?" she asked him after he finished speaking.

"Well, I was hoping you could give me some advice," he said.

"All right, so let me ask you this: How do you want the conversation to turn out? And what is your mindset right now?"

Dan's anger was starting to surface. "In the next two hours there's going to be a one-sided conversation, and Jude is going to be fired. That's how the conversation is going to turn out. I'm so furious over all this. My God, he was trying to arrange the sale of this company right out from under our noses. He could have taken down the entire operation, and —"

Michelle interrupted politely. "So I repeat my question, Dan: How do you want this conversation to turn out?" He fell silent, and Michelle continued. "You have lots of options. Do you want revenge? Do you want to put him down and make him feel demeaned? You're at a crossroads with Jude, and you get to decide what path you're going to take."

"I want him to suffer for all the harm he's done to me and to my relationship with Dad," Dan said immediately. "I want him to pay for what he was doing to bring down this company. I want everyone in the company to know the kind of person he really is. I want to expose this loser for the incompetent and conniving slime bag he really is."

"That's understandable," Michelle said. "But don't forget, Dan, that your entire company will eventually find out how you handle this. There are no secrets. What sort of example do you want to set? This is another defining moment for you as a leader. You create your legacy every day through your attitude and actions. What do you want your employees and customers to say about you once they hear about how this all went down?"

That question halted Dan's seething anger in its tracks. He hadn't thought about it that way.

Michelle continued. "You heard what I told the sales team. Nothing escapes the consequences of our thoughts, feelings, actions, or words. Is that environment of anger and payback truly what you want to create?"

She was exactly right. Thank goodness he had called Michelle before meeting with Jude.

"I don't know what I was thinking," Dan told her. "Regardless of what Jude has done, it's up to me as a leader to take the high road. I'm going to handle this with the utmost professionalism, calm, and gravity. I'll treat him the way I would want to be treated if the tables were turned."

"Good," Michelle said approvingly.

"But God help him if he interprets my professionalism and calmness for weakness!" Dan added.

He thanked Michelle for being available at short notice and talking him through the situation.

"That's why I'm here, Dan. I'm your confidential sounding board. And by the way, I gave you no advice. You had all the answers. My job is simply to ask the questions in order for you find them."

Dan had just ended his conversation with Michelle when Will knocked on his office door.

"I have a couple of things for you. First, Charlie did some more digging and got the proof we were looking for. You were being undermined. And therefore, the fact that Jude would be going around you — to the bank, to a potential buyer — and causing the bank to lose confidence in you and the company is a fiduciary breach. You could sue him.

"And second, I just got off the phone with Phil Oberrecht, our legal counsel. He asked that you call him before talking with Jude. Phil's a good guy and he and your father go way back."

"Good, because I have a few questions to ask him myself," Dan replied.

"Are you sure you want to do this one alone, Dan? Nothing would give me greater satisfaction than taking that underhanded little sucker down."

"No, Will," Dan said. "This has been a long time coming, and I know exactly what I need to do."

"Then best of luck," Will said, and left, closing Dan's office door behind him.

Dan picked up the phone and called the company attorney.

CHAPTER SEVENTEEN

LATER THAT AFTERNOON, DAN TAPPED ON THE door to Jude's office and looked in. "Do you have a few minutes to talk?" he asked.

Jude was sitting at his desk surrounded by papers. "As you can see, I'm really busy," he said tonelessly, not looking away from his computer screen. "I'm sure whatever you have to say can wait until tomorrow."

"Actually, Jude, it can't," Dan said. He opened the door all the way and walked in. Phil Oberrecht followed him. When Jude saw Phil, his faced drained of color.

"What's going on? Why is he here?" he demanded.

"I have a few things to ask you, Jude," Dan said, trying carefully to keep his tone even. "I've been presented with evidence that you have been working behind my back to orchestrate the sale of this business to another company. That other company is our major competitor. Is this true, Jude?"

Phil stood there silently. Jude's eyes darted from one expressionless face to another. "What are you — I don't know what you're talking about, Dan!" he spluttered. "What are you accusing me of? Do you think I would ever do anything like that? You have to be out of your mind! You're crazy — just like your sister says. A stark raving idiot."

Dan held up a hand. "Be careful, Jude. Name-calling isn't necessary. I'm absolutely clear on what I'm asking, and I assure you I'm not out of my mind." Dan felt calm, in control, and stronger than he'd felt in years.

"You have no proof!" Jude said. "This is slander. I'll sue you for defamation of character before all this is over. I promise you."

"It's not my intention to slander you," Dan said. "I just want the truth from you, in your own words. Phil and I wouldn't be here right now if we didn't have actual proof of what you've been up to."

Jude was silent, but hatred like Dan had never seen before filled his face. For a few seconds, Jude simply glared. Then he spoke. "You want the truth? Well, here it is, Danny Boy. The truth is your father never believed in you. I know that. Everyone here knows that. You are nothing, Dan.

"You came here to work out of graduate school so full of yourself. You acted so superior to the rest of us when you first started here. All those big ideas. Your arrogance was too much for any of us to take. You should be ashamed of the way you treated Mike…and all of us. All the ridiculous ideas and changes you were trying to cram down our throats. Are you honestly surprised that Mike didn't want you taking over meetings with your business school talk?

"Then you come in here after Mike died thinking you could take over this company he built. It's like I said — you're going to run this company into the ground. You don't know what you're doing. You have no clue how to run a company like this. I knew sooner than later that you would ruin this company because of your incompetence and your ego. So I decided to take matters into my own hands for the good of this company."

Dan felt his face burning at Jude's words, but knew the next part was crucial. "So it is true then that you have been working with Bridger Landscaping to orchestrate the sale of this company?" he asked.

"Yes, it is!" Jude snapped. "And I honestly believe that's what Mike would have wanted, too. It was never his intention to have you run this place. Abby has even told me that."

"So are you saying Abby knew about this, too?"

"Well, no. But all she wants is her inheritance and to cut any ties she ever had to this place. She was never part of this business and has no intention of being a part of it — now or ever."

"Is it true that once the sale was complete that you would be the new CEO?" Dan asked.

"Hell, yes, it is, and I would do a far better job running it than you could ever imagine doing!" Jude stopped, breathing heavily, and stared defiantly at Dan.

Dan took a breath. Then he said, matter-of-factly, "Well, I'm sorry, Jude, but that's not going to happen. Here's what *is* going to happen. There are some cardboard boxes outside your office door. You are going to use them to pack up the personal items from your office. Phil and I are going to stand here and watch you do it. Once you're done packing up your office, you'll be escorted to your car, through the back entrance to be as discreet as possible."

As Dan spoke, Jude's eyes got bigger, his face redder. Dan next turned to Phil. "Phil, would you please hand me the document we discussed this afternoon?"

"Here it is," said Phil, reaching into his briefcase and handing Dan a folder. Dan opened the folder and pulled out a document, which he held out to Jude, who didn't take it. Dan laid it on the desk facing Jude.

"Do you recall signing this last summer — July 23, to be exact?"

Jude actually seemed to stop breathing momentarily. His eyes registered shock and disbelief. "How did you find out about this? Mike didn't even tell Will about this. He said he wouldn't."

"That's why companies have legal counsel," Phil interjected in a barely audible tone. Dan glanced at the always-deadpan attorney and thought he detected just a hint of a smile.

"So you're just firing me? YOU'RE firing ME?" By now Jude was yelling loud enough for half the hallway to hear. Reality was starting to sink in. "If you fire me, Dan, I promise I am going to take you down. You mark my words. I will take you down." He paused between each word slowly and deliberately. "I'm going to see to it that Bridger buries you once and for all."

"I don't think that's going to happen, Jude," Phil said. "Last summer you signed the non-compete agreement you're holding in your hand. Mike came to me citing concerns about you that are not relevant to this discussion, and said he wanted to make sure if you were ever to leave or be fired, Richards' wouldn't suffer for it. I advised him to have you sign this non-compete agreement. It is written to legal perfection, so it is basically bulletproof. And it's valid for five years, whether you decide to leave or are terminated with cause."

"This is absolute lunacy!" Jude shouted. "I've given years to this company. Your mother would roll over in her grave if she knew what you were doing, Dan. This company is as good as failed already."

"Let's not bring my mother into this, if you don't mind. Everything has consequences, Jude, and I'm confident that once we do some more digging, we're going to find more improprieties," Dan said. Then he softened his tone a bit. "Listen, you're family. You've been with the company for a long time, and you worked with my father. I give you my word that if you simply leave now peacefully and cause no further problems, I will not take legal action against you." Dan was grateful to have Phil there as a witness.

Jude didn't say anything, so Dan opened the office door and began bringing in the empty boxes, which he set down next to the desk. He noticed several of the administrative assistants watching from their desks. Most looked shocked; one was texting rapidly. Dan closed the door again, and he and Phil sat as Jude began scooping up his personal items and dumping them into the boxes.

"We know you have a company laptop at your home, and I want you to know that as we speak, your business files are being taken off your system. If we discover that any information has been leaked in any way to any company — well, to use Dan's words, there will be consequences," Phil said. "What questions do you have?"

Jude again didn't reply and continued to throw his things into the boxes. After what appeared to be the last of it was packed up, Dan stood. "Well, I guess that's it," he said. Jude didn't acknowledge him. Dan turned and headed for the door, then stopped and turned back. He couldn't help but ask one last question. "Why?" he said. "Why did you do this, Jude?"

To his surprise, Jude stopped what he was doing and looked at him, making eye contact for the first time since he'd started packing.

"Why?" He straightened up and squared his shoulders. "I'll tell you why. I obviously have nothing more to lose."

He paused, then said almost cockily, "This all was calculated. Mike's heart was no longer in the business after Aunt Rita died. Everyone knew it. It's like he didn't even care about where we were financially. So I took it upon myself to have another company waiting in the wings to take over once the bank shut the company off. It was the perfect scenario. The bank would be happy because I had found a buyer, Mike could retire and get out of this whole mess, you and Abby would walk away with your inheritance, and I'd take over as president."

He paused again, and said, "Then Mike goes and dies. And you get in the way of everything."

Dan said nothing. There was nothing to say. This was almost unbearable to hear. His mind would not allow him to think right now about everything that could be different had Jude actually worked with his father rather than doing what he'd done. As utterly painful as it was to hear all this, he understood that knowing the truth was the only way he could ever hope to accept it and get closure.

Thankfully, Will had arranged to have a cart waiting outside Jude's office to haul the boxes to his car. Phil and Dan stood in the parking lot watching as Jude loaded the boxes into the back of his SUV. Dan offered to help, but the look of disgust on Jude's face said it all. Jude got in, slammed the door, and took off so fast the tires squealed on the pavement.

Dan sighed. "Thanks for all your help, Phil," he said as he walked Phil to his car.

They shook hands, and Phil said, "I'm sorry it had to come to this. No one wins in situations like this. You seem like a good guy with a lot of potential. You did an unbelievable job controlling yourself in that meeting. You had plenty of opportunities to unload on him, and you didn't. That showed a tremendous amount of class and maturity. I look forward to getting to know you better. By the way, your bill for this one is on me. I never cared for the guy." He smiled and waved as he drove off.

Dan headed back to his office and found Will and Charlie waiting in the hallway for an update.

"It went as well as could be expected," Dan told them. "Phil informed me of Jude's non-compete agreement right before our meeting and brought a copy of it with him. I honestly believe Jude thought that little secret had died with Dad."

As they went over the details of everything, Dan realized something. "Maybe Jude's original intentions could've had some good in them," he said. "But it's amazing how the human mind has the ability to rationalize anything. Almost all embezzlers can rationalize their actions."

Shaking his head Will said, "Mike was losing interest in the business. His friends were retiring. Rita was gone. What did he have to look forward to? So Jude started asking around to see if anyone had an interest in buying Richards'. As things then seemed to progress, he started to see his potential for personal and financial gain, and his actions began to take on a life of their own. Power, greed, and deception took over."

Then Will said, "We have a challenging situation on our hands with Jude out of the picture. We have the bank to think about. Jude basically controlled the banking relationship for the past two years."

Charlie had been quiet, and looked deep in thought. Now he spoke up. "Before our next meeting with the bank we need to know exactly where we stand. I have the perfect guy in mind to go through the books and help us prepare for our meeting. He can also help us find a replacement for Jude."

"Sounds great, Charlie," Dan said. All of a sudden he felt exhausted. "I don't know about you two, but it's been a rough day and I'm beat. How about if we call it a day and reconvene in the morning?"

"Sounds good," Charlie said. "I think I can still make my dinner reservation for tonight." He stood up and stretched. "Good job handling this, Dan," he said. "See you both in the morning."

After he left, Will stood up too. "You did yourself proud today, Dan. Without challenge, there can be no greatness." He patted Dan on the shoulder, then turned to leave. "Get some rest, and I'll see you in the morning."

"Will, wait," Dan said quickly. "Something else Jude said is stuck in my mind. And the very thought of it makes me sick. Do you have a few more minutes to talk?"

CHAPTER EIGHTEEN

WILL SAT BACK DOWN IN THE DESK CHAIR AND looked at Dan.

Dan sat down too. "Listen, you know me as well as anyone here. You remember when I first came to work here, don't you?"

"Of course I do, Dan. Why?"

"Today was an especially tough day in a lot of ways. I'm the kind of guy who's more extraverted and likes to talk over things that are on my mind. I find it easier to think that way. Here's what's really gnawing at me. Ever since I took over Dad's position it's been tough, and the reality and magnitude of what Jude was doing is only now starting to soak in. I can't believe something like this was going on right under our noses. But of all the things Jude said to me this afternoon, there's something that's thrown me for a loop." He paused, emotions threatening to flood out and choke him. He looked down at the floor and ran his fingers through his hair.

"What is it, Dan?" Will asked, concerned. "Tell me what's going on."

"It's something Jude said about me…and Dad. And I think…" He tried to get the words out. Will waited silently for him to continue.

"Jude said that when I started working here after business school that I was an arrogant ass with a pompous attitude — nobody could stand me. He said I was the worst toward Dad… and that's why Dad and everyone treated me the way they did, just constantly writing me off. Is that true?"

This was difficult for him to say — and to admit. "Was I really that bad? Did I really treat Dad that way?"

Will could tell that a lot of issues had begun to surface.

"First of all, Dan, consider the source. Jude knew if you decided to institute change around here and were successful, his plan to take your job would never work. And let's face it — he's had it in for you for years. Who knows why — jealously, insecurity, rivalry, competition, whatever. It doesn't matter now. He has his own issues to deal with.

"Second, do I think you treated your dad disrespectfully back then? Yeah, I guess sometimes you did. But I knew you were frustrated, but it was never to the extent you're thinking. You were a passionate young guy fresh out of school. You wanted to try your wings. You'd been waiting to get into the game here since you were a kid, like you said. And right off the bat you were benched.

"When you first started here, you were so full of enthusiasm and eager to change things for the better. Mike and I had a number of private conversations about your ideas. Several I thought were quite good, but Mike thought they were too risky. You know your dad was not one who embraced change very well. His whole philosophy was, 'Why upset the applecart?'

"You and Mike were about as opposite as two people could be. Mike was quiet, reserved, and liked sameness and routine. He was a control freak. And you…you're outgoing, you say what's on your mind, you're an out-of-the-box thinker, a consensus-builder, and a calculated risk-taker. You embrace change. It was a classic case of oil and water.

"But Mike was in control and had no desire to relinquish it in any way — even to me. You and I had several talks about your dad back then. You knew I had my frustrations, too.

"And here's one I don't think you know. Mike never said this, but I always believed he was pretty intimidated by your education. He could've gone on to college after he was turned down to go into the service, but he chose not to. He and your mother met, and his next step was to get married and go to work here. Parents are human, too — they're not immune to jealousy, insecurity, or rivalry."

Dan had to interrupt. "But I can't help thinking — what if I hadn't been like that? What if I had talked with Dad about my business ideas differently? What if I hadn't been such an arrogant ass? What if Dad had agreed to try even one or two of my ideas — would we be in the situation we're in today? What if we could have gotten over our egos and gotten to be friends and partners — would he have died so early? You have no idea how much I just wanted Dad to be a friend. My dream had always been that someday we'd work together as partners, not adversaries. The very thought that I could be partially responsible for the stress and suffering Dad experienced before he died is unbearable. I should have tried to be a better son. I should've been there more for him after Mom died, but he wouldn't let me in."

Dan stopped, his eyes burning, the lump in his throat feeling like a golf ball.

Will had been listening intently as Dan spoke. Then he said, "Dan, here are a few more what ifs. What if your Dad had tried one or two of your ideas? What if they hadn't worked? What if there was more going on in your dad's life than you know about that contributed to his early death? What if your dad just got tired of living without your mother and wanted out? What if the responsibility of his death isn't yours?"

Dan tried his best to keep his composure, but his eyes, as they so often had lately, filled with tears. "But now he's just gone, and I can't tell you how much I still miss him. Yes, he frustrated the hell out of me and made me furious sometimes, but I never stopped loving him. And that's what hurts so much. He never once told me he loved me…until the night he died."

Dan kept talking, years of pent-up resentment spilling out of him. "Grandfather was a real son of a bitch toward him, too — the same way he was to me. Grandfather thought that being hard on Dad would toughen him up. But it just turned him into a son of a bitch, too. Maybe that's why Dad was so rough on me. Who the hell knows?" His voice cracked. "I don't know what to do," he said sadly.

Will reached across the desk to touch his arm. "Maybe Mike wanted you to take what you learned from your grandfather and him — the good and not so good — and start fresh.

"There's a saying that says, 'Forgiveness is the giving, and so the receiving.' We can't change our past, but we can change our attitude toward it. None of us will ever escape the lessons life has in store for us. It's in experiencing these tough life lessons that we learn and grow the most. Forgiveness and understanding start from within.

"It's a state of understanding the other person and their reasons for their behavior so clearly that you can say, in all honesty, that there is nothing more to forgive. Seek to understand, and you will find that little by little, understanding will come to you."

"But how do I do that?" Dan asked, still feeling lost.

"You're on the right path. You have people around you who aren't going to let you or this company fail. You've had a really rough day — hell, you've had a rough month, for that matter. You're exhausted. Go home and get some rest. Tomorrow we'll figure out what our next steps are. It's like FDR said: 'When you've come to the end of your rope, tie a knot and hang on!'"

Will was right. It was impossible to think logically when in a state of physical, mental, and emotional exhaustion. He gave Will a weak smile and promised he'd get some rest.

He felt too exhausted for the gym that night, especially since it was cold and pouring rain again. Instead he called and asked Vince to come over and watch football. Ever since college they'd had an understanding that whatever they spoke about would stay between them, and Dan knew he could let down his guard. A few beers, football, Mully, and his best friend were just what he needed that night.

Before going to bed he decided to check his email one last time. He was surprised to see a new message from his sister. He clicked on it and began to read.

Dan,

I just heard the news about Jude and decided it's time to write to you. It's no big secret that I've been doing my best to avoid you since Dad died. Jude contacted me from time to time, and as you might guess, what he was writing about you was pretty bad. I now know he was poison and was cheating the family.

Let's face it, Dan. You and I are completely different people. I couldn't wait to get out of town fast enough after high school, and you couldn't wait to get back home after college and work at the company. I know how committed you are to making it work despite everything. And now this awful news about Jude. I never dreamed he could be capable of such deception.

I feel I should tell you some things about the business and our family. The first is that I have always hated and resented that damn place. In my mind it robbed us of our childhoods, and our parents — especially Dad. Our lives were consumed by that damned place, and I grew to hate it. That's why I got involved in sports, music, gymnastics — anything just so I didn't have to go home, which was empty most of the time. We always knew we were loved and financially supported, but Mom and Dad were never really there for me — or for you. I feel like I raised myself. Thank God Grams was always there for us.

You've always had this ability to stay positive regardless of what was thrown at you. I admired that about you, and I was jealous of it, too. I'm not wired that way. I'm competitive and really not a team player. I knew I could never compete with you at the business. You are a leader, and you always have been.

I have a lot of regrets about my past, with Mom and Dad... and you. I never really understood or appreciated you, and I'm sorry for that. I'm still trying to come to terms with the past and let it heal. I think Gandhi had it right when he wrote, "The weak can never forgive. Forgiveness is the attribute of the strong."

Jonathan and I have our own lives to think about now. I will support whatever decisions you make with the company, but know that long-term, I still want out. I'll never feel connected to that company like you do. I understand what Richards' means to you, and I'll stop fighting you over it. I've called off the dogs. All I ask is that you keep me in the loop over what's going on.

Abby

Dan was floored. In just one day he'd fired his cousin and expressed all his innermost fears to Will, and now his sister was waving a white flag. Things were moving forward rapidly, even though Dan felt like he'd spent the past month mired in memories.

As he crawled into bed, he remembered a quote from Lily Tomlin that an old college girlfriend had told him: "Forgiveness means giving up all hope for a better past." Dan realized it was time for him to let go and stop holding on to what might have been.

CHAPTER NINETEEN

THE NEXT MORNING, DAN GOT UP EARLY AND headed to the gym near his house to meet Vince and a couple of their other workout buddies before he went to the office. Thanks to his coaching with Michelle, he'd gotten back into his workout routine again. It was helpful having someone to hold him accountable for doing what he said he was going to do. He had shed those unwanted pounds and was starting to feel good again. And it was nice to reconnect with his old friends. At least that part of his life was showing progress.

When Dan got to the office he headed to the kitchen for some coffee and ran into Will. "Charlie's on his way here," Will said. "He told me he has some news, but he didn't say what about. I told him to meet us in your office."

Charlie arrived shortly after. "I didn't tell you what I was doing last night because I wasn't sure about what I was going to hear," he said as he settled into one of the chairs in front of Dan's desk.

"Oh, God. What's up now?" Dan asked, feeling extremely apprehensive.

"I'm just going to get right to it. Last night I had dinner with Grant Evans from Bridger Landscaping."

"Charlie, what in the world are you talking about?" Will said.

"You know Grant? You had dinner with him?" Dan asked.

"Yes, I did, and I was the one who asked for the meeting. I've known Grant vaguely through the country club, and I wanted to hear from him exactly what was going on and just how far these discussions had gone with Jude. Grant had already heard he'd been fired.

"Well, what did he have to say?" asked Will.

"It boils down to this: Bridger still wants to buy Richards," Charlie said.

Dan's mouth dropped open. Charlie continued. "But there is good news and bad news. The good news is that the offer is a good one, practically unheard of in today's market. With that kind of money, your life would be golden — Abby's, too. But the bad news, Dan, is that you'd be out. They want to change the direction of this company and merge it into Bridger's entire operation. Grant said it would be an ideal fit for them."

Will blew out a long breath. "This is pretty amazing news, Charlie. So I assume they want to bring in their own management team."

Charlie nodded. "Without Jude, of course."

As Charlie and Will continued to discuss the potential deal, Dan turned away and looked out of the window overlooking the garden center. He saw employees getting ready to open the store shortly. Then he turned to the right and looked at the pictures on his credenza of his grandfather, his dad, their family — pictures collected over the past seven decades.

This was an unbelievable opportunity, he thought to himself. Anyone would be a fool to turn this down. But the Richards weren't just anyone.

"Dan?" he heard Will say. He turned back around to face them. "What are you thinking?" Will asked.

Dan glanced at the picture of his grandfather again. Then he said, "In these past months I've learned more about my grandfather than I ever knew. He was an amazing guy. Even with an eighth-grade education, he valued learning. He was an avid reader and a pretty great writer. He wrote several things in his journal that I hope I'll never forget. One was that 'great challenge bares the truth of a person's worth.' Another was that 'every adversity carries the seed of an equal or greater benefit.' I can see you both looking at me like I'd be crazy not to consider Grant's offer. But I can't. I have a responsibility to those people out there," he said, pointing out the window, "and to their families. I can't just sell this place.

"I know there has to be another way to keep this company going without having to sell. There has to be. Accepting Grant's offer is an easy way out for sure, but I don't want to do what's easy. I want to do what's right — what's right for this amazing legacy that's been handed down to me and for all these hundreds of people and families who have depended on us for generations. This isn't just about Abby and me anymore. It's about them, too. There has to be another way to make this work without selling."

Charlie was first to speak. "There are options for you, Dan. One is bringing in a private equity group. I know several that would jump at the opportunity to invest in this company."

Dan couldn't interrupt fast enough. "That's not an option, Charlie. I know all about them, and I'm adamant that no one outside this company will own a piece of it if I can help it. Grandfather and Dad faced their own adversities and I'm going to get through this with this company intact. What else?"

Charlie looked at Will and then to Dan. "Here's what I suggest, then. We have to get things settled here before we can consider anything else. Set another meeting with Frank at the bank. With Jude gone, we need to reassure him that you have things under control."

Will added, "And we need to get our arms around our financials once and for all. We need to know where we stand regarding our loan covenants with the bank."

Charlie added, "Dan, before you turn this offer down, meet with the bank to see where the company stands with them. You still need that bank loan; otherwise, you are going to have to take the offer."

Dan told them he would call Frank right away and get a meeting scheduled.

Luckily, that afternoon Dan had a coaching appointment with Michelle. There was so much to discuss with her today. Where to start?

Michelle arrived promptly at two o'clock. Twenty-five minutes later Dan finally stopped talking. She sat patiently and listened to him tell about Jude and the possible offer from Bridger. She then said, "From what you described, selling to Bridger could solve your financial problems. But would it solve everything else?"

"What do you mean?"

Michelle opened her coaching notebook and said, "Not too long ago, I asked you what you ultimately wanted to have in your life. Do you remember what you said? You told me you wanted to find your voice. You also said you wanted to redeem your personal and professional reputation — to prove yourself to your family, friends, and employees that you could successfully lead this company.

"So considering that, how do you see yourself going forward now?"

Dan told her about his upcoming meeting at the bank. "But it's not just this financial mess that's bothering me. Since I took over as CEO, all I've done is put out fires. We still have no direction or plan for this company. I wrote an entire business plan for Richards' some years ago for Dad and this company. And we know what that got me!"

"Tell me more about what you created," Michelle said.

Dan pulled up the files on his computer. "Here it is. I suggested a vision and mission statement, specific strategies…and look at this — here are all the goals and action plans to guide the daily, weekly, and monthly actions per department."

"Could you read me the mission statement you created for Richards'?"   Michelle asked.

Dan sat up a bit in his chair and cleared his throat. "It still needs work, but here's what I wrote: 'In a spirit of family tradition, enthusiasm, and passion, Richards' is dedicated to creating a culture of partnership with our employees, suppliers, and valued customers, and to providing the highest-quality service, support, and materials at a fair and honest price. We gladly share our generations of knowledge, skill, and expertise for those seeking to enhance quality of life through gardening and outdoor living.'"

He looked up, and joked, "I wanted it to be, 'Come play in the dirt with us,' but it was already taken!" Michelle laughed.

"It appears you already have a lot created that you can use. What's your next step with all this?"

"Georgia is in the process of helping me coordinate a company offsite meeting. Will and Charlie already have copies of this business plan. Among other things, I plan to review it at the meeting to get the team's input. And we can use this information to show the bank that we have strategies and plans in place going forward."

"Speaking of that, have you thought any more about how you see yourself as a leader?"

"I've actually written quite a lot about this," Dan said taking his journal out of his side drawer. He began reading. "I want to be an authentic and values-driven leader. I want to do what's right rather than what's popular. In the aftermath of all that's happened on Wall Street and in the political arena, I want to be a leader with a deep sense of honesty, guts, and integrity, and stay true to my personal and organizational core values.

"I want people to work here because they want to be here and want to make a difference, not just bring home a paycheck. I want all employees to feel like Richards' is their company. I want to build a strong sense of community with everyone. I want these employees to respect me and feel comfortable coming to me if they disagree with me. I want two-way communication at all times. I'm committed to learning, because I believe that becoming a leader takes a lifetime."

Michelle said, "You're off to an excellent start. I'd like to suggest that you continue to think about how you can drive this into your organization. Think about what traits and skills you'll need to develop within yourself and your leadership team to make this part of the overall culture here."

Dan nodded. Then Michelle said, "On a slightly different topic, you sent me an email the other day asking about nepotism and entitlement. They are significant issues here — most recently with Jude, and with Keith and Samantha in sales. Before I left the office, I sent you an email pertaining to that with some information you may find helpful with some recommended reading.

"And one more thing before we conclude. I'm putting on my consultant hat now. I have a suggestion for you, if you don't mind." She glanced at her notes for a minute, then back at Dan.

"Listening to the mission statement you wrote for this company, it sounds like your employees are an integral part of your vision and success. You have a lot of options for how to best do that. Has Charlie ever mentioned employee ownership? It's grown significantly in popularity over the past decade. He's the expert on this, but an employee stock ownership plan (ESOP) allows your employees to be stockholders in the company. It's not for every type of business and depends on the structure of the company, but you might consider asking him about it. You did say you were adamant no one outside this company will own a piece of it. Perhaps your employees hold the answers. And it could be a possible way to buy Abby out of the company."

"That would be amazing," Dan said, making a mental note to bring up ESOPS with Charlie at his earliest opportunity.

After Michelle left, Dan leaned back in his chair, again looking out the window. There was still so much to figure out, so many problems to resolve, but at least Jude could no longer undermine him, and Abby had decided to get off his back and support him.

Dan turned back to his desk and opened his email program. There was a message from Michelle with the subject line: Nepotism, Entitlement, and Mentoring.

Dan:

Nepotism is nearly impossible to avoid and is very common in family owned companies — look at the Trump organization. After all, who better to take over than those already in the inner circle?

Your company employs people from all over the area, and you cannot avoid having relatives working together. Nepotism should be an acknowledged and hard-wired part of the business. It is possible to make it work with plans and structures in place.

A longstanding client recently shared this with me. In order to keep new life and innovation going in his particular family-owned company, the owner made an announcement to every person there — especially to all family members and friends. It stated that before anyone would be considered for a management position, he or she must have had at least two years of outside work experience. The owner made it clear that just because someone interviewing for a management position was family or a friend, they were not entitled to anything. Everything was to be earned.

And finally, you asked about mentoring programs. I have helped create them for a number of companies over the past few years, and, when done correctly, mentoring programs can really make a difference. Just let me know if you want more information and how I might help.

Michelle

Dan hit the Reply button to thank Michelle for this information. But before he hit Send, he thought about his time so far working with her. There were already significant differences in his life and Dan wanted to tell Michelle how much he sincerely appreciated her and their work together.

He thought back to those original six questions from Michelle's website that asked whether executive coaching was the right fit. There was no question that coaching was already bringing about positive change in his life. There had been things he wanted to change but didn't know how, and with her help, he was making those changes. As the days and weeks passed, he felt more and more like he was getting his life back in balance and his priorities in line. Michelle had helped him navigate some pretty difficult situations and conversations. She had also helped him reignite his creative juices and regain his confidence. Because of their work together, Dan was learning the real meaning of commitment, accountability, and, most of all, leadership. He put those feelings of thanks and gratitude into the message and hit Send.

Then Dan called Will and Charlie. They had to put their full effort into this next meeting with the bank. The fate of the business depended on this meeting.

CHAPTER TWENTY

CHARLIE, WILL, AND DAN HAD PLANNED TO meet in Dan's office for a few more hours before leaving that night. They wanted to once again thoroughly review every piece of documentation that had been presented to the bank at their last meeting.

"If we're out of compliance on simply one thing, the bank can pull the loan," Charlie said, looking down at the latest reports. "But from the looks of everything, you are in compliance. You have maintained proper and accurate up-to-date reports of financial performance and condition. The only thing that has me confused is the cash-flow accounting. There seem to be some key pieces of information still in question."

"And Jude had his hands all over that," Dan said with a sinking feeling.

About that time Kent Mills, the temporary accounting expert Charlie had hired for Richards', knocked on the door to Dan's office.

"Kent, please come in," Charlie said. Kent was carrying a pile of folders. "Have a seat."

"Gentlemen, let me tell you the situation," Kent began. "For at least two years, Jude has been manipulating the finances of this company. In the last annual audited statement, two years ago there were questions raised by the auditing firm about not taking cash discounts. My preliminary audit shows that that practice, which reduces profits, has continued." He handed a copy of the financial statements he was referencing to each of them.

"Until a year ago, the bank was satisfied with the annual statements. But since the beginning of this year, there's been a consistent drop in profits and a deterioration of the balance sheet. Because of declining financial conditions, the bank had been requiring monthly financial statements."

As Kent spoke, a few things about Dan's dad were beginning to make more sense. This past year Dan had noticed changes in Mike. His temper, always short, had begun to flare up at a hair trigger, he'd started smoking again, and he'd gained quite a few pounds. Dan realized those were all signs of stress — and that, combined with the unhealthy habits he'd lapsed into, must have strained his heart.

"This is interesting," he told the group. "Two years ago, Steve Giles, Dad's longtime associate and president of the bank decided to retire...and that's when Frank Wilson came onboard with Richards'. Dad had already begun losing interest in the company and didn't care to develop a relationship with Frank, who was a lot younger than Steve; Dad felt he had nothing in common with him. So Jude stepped in. Dad put all his trust in Jude, and Jude saw it as an opportunity to begin to manipulate the company's finances."

Kent said, "Jude ran down your working capital. As far as I can tell, he allowed approximately $100,000 of profits to slip away by not taking advantage of cash discounts for timely payments. I know Jude said you didn't have the cash flow to do it, but that's incorrect. He was financing equipment purchases through your line of credit. He put this company out of compliance, but it doesn't need to be."

Dan looked up from the report he was studying.

"What did you just say, Kent?" he asked in amazement.

"It's all there," Kent said, pointing at the reports. "By simply taking advantage of the cash discounts, the profitability would have improved by $100,000. Companies need to manage their payables correctly, or things like this can and do happen."

Dan couldn't believe his ears. Will and Charlie looked similarly shocked.

"My suggestion is that when you meet with the bank, ask to get equipment loans on these particular items you purchased. Then tell the bank that with your credit line and by taking discounts, you can increase the profitability by at least $100,000."

Kent opened another folder and pointed to another large spreadsheet. "It shows here that Mike was taking a healthy yearly salary. It also shows that you, Dan, reduced your salary to $50,000 — a significant cut."

Will's eyebrows lifted. "I didn't know you cut your own salary," he said, turning to Dan.

"I couldn't justify taking any more than that once I learned about our financial predicament," Dan said. "I made those changes several weeks ago. And any bonuses I take will be based on profitability."

"You didn't mention that to me," Will said still surprised.

"I decided that my compensation should be based on the profitability of this company. If our employees have to earn it, so do I."

Charlie cut in. "So if my calculations are correct, Richards' actually should have made money last year? With Mike's salary gone and Dan's decrease in salary, along with picking up $100,000 in discounts, we will show a defined increase in profitability."

Dan turned to Kent and asked, "Then from the looks of everything, it might not be as bad as we thought?"

Kent said, "It appears that way, Dan. But we aren't out of the woods yet."

Will put down the notes he had been taking. "I find this all absolutely amazing," he said. "Jude didn't really do anything illegal, but he was choking the company with working capital. He made sure we didn't have enough money in our line of credit because he was using it elsewhere — to finance our equipment. We could have had a separate loan for that. And because of that, there was not enough working capital available to take advantage of the early payment discounts. Instead, he cost this company at least $100,000."

Kent then said, "But the good news, gentlemen, is that financially speaking, you do not have a problem." It was music to Dan's ears.

"You know you could pursue legal action towards Jude for what he's done, right?" Kent said, looking curiously at Dan. "He's caused you harm with his improper use of cash."

That comment set Will off. "You're damn right he could, Kent. Jude's a cold-blooded crook, and I want that SOB exposed for what he's done!"

Charlie looked surprised at the outburst. Dan tried to calm Will down. "I understand what you're saying, but I told Jude I wouldn't proceed with any legal action as long as he left the company peacefully and we don't ever hear from him again. I intend to honor that promise.

"I recently read, 'There is no revenge so complete as forgiveness.' I plan to take this company forward, not backward, and entering into a lawsuit now isn't what I want for this company… or for me. Bridger won't hire him. In fact, after word gets out about all this, I can't image anyone around here will. He's poison, to quote my sister. And he knows that if at any time he doesn't honor his end of the deal, I have Phil, our legal counsel, locked and loaded to go after him. As far as I'm concerned, once we get the financial situation resolved, we're starting a brand new chapter here at Richards.'"

"Well, there you have it," Charlie said, turning to Will, who nodded. "Thanks for all your help, Kent," Dan said, shaking his hand as he left.

The meeting at the bank was tomorrow at one o'clock, and Will, Charlie, and Dan decided to block off the whole afternoon. Not knowing how long — or brief — the meeting would be, it seemed like the right thing to do.

Dan was up most of the night thinking about the bank meeting. When he got to the office the next morning he decided to make a phone call. It was to Bill Miller, the president of the bank. He didn't tell Will or Charlie of his plan.

He dialed the phone and got Bill's assistant, who put him through right away.

"Hello, Mr. Miller? This is Dan Richards. I am with — "

"I know exactly who you're with," Bill interrupted. "What can I do for you, Mr. Richards?"

Chapter Twenty-One

"I'LL GET RIGHT TO THE POINT, MR. MILLER," Dan said. "The reason for this call is to open up the lines of communication with each other. I don't know if you know this, but your predecessor, Steve Giles, dealt exclusively with my father. When Mr. Giles retired, Frank Wilson took over our account, and our CFO has been doing business with him.

"I've recently become privy to some knowledge about our CFO, and while I am not accusing the bank of any improprieties, I am requesting that Richards' be assigned a new representative."

There was a slight pause at the other end of the phone. Then Bill said, "I'm very aware that Richards' has been a long and loyal customer of ours. If memory serves me, our relationship goes back even further — to your grandfather in the 1940s.

Dan, I would like to personally handle your account. And please, call me Bill."

Dan hadn't expected that. "I would like that very much. Thank you, Bill," he said. He informed Bill of the meeting at the bank later that afternoon, and after exchanging a couple more pleasantries, they hung up.

Dan thought the phone call was a step in a positive direction. He was as prepared as he could possibly be for the meeting that afternoon. And he felt mentally and physically good. He was getting back into shape again. And on Michelle's gentle recommendation, he had gotten a much-needed haircut.

The week before, at their coaching session, she reminded him of the importance of dressing for success. "Only seven percent of what we communicate is through our words, Dan," she said. "Think about what you want to communicate through your executive image."

So Dan had purchased a sharp new suit, a crisp white shirt, a new tie, and a new pair of shoes, all of which he donned for the bank meeting. He felt fully confident and ready.

Frank Wilson's secretary greeted Dan, Charlie, and Will when they arrived at the bank that afternoon and invited them into the conference room next to Frank's office.

After some brief small talk, Dan began the meeting, addressing Frank. "Have you ever heard the old Yiddish proverb that says, 'A half truth is a whole lie'? Jude Perry was responsible for managing the financial interests of Richards' and for providing truthful and accurate financial information. And since Dad died, I've been at his mercy."

Frank opened his mouth to reply, but at that moment the door to the conference room opened and in walked a tall, distinguished-looking man with wavy hair, dressed in an extremely polished charcoal gray suit, white shirt, and light blue tie. His gold metal nametag read William Miller. Frank's mouth fell open, and he quickly stood up to greet his boss. Dan also stood, and held his hand out to Bill, who shook it.

"Hello, Bill. I'm Dan Richards. And these are my colleagues." Will and Charlie shook Bill's hand, as well.

"It's a pleasure to meet you, gentlemen," Bill said. "I heard about this meeting and decided to sit in if you don't mind, Frank. I believe I'm up to speed on everything associated with the Richards' account. Please continue."

Everyone sat down again, and Dan continued. "After our last meeting, the three of us knew something was wrong from the way you were acting, Frank, but had no way of knowing what. We asked Jude, who was also there, if he noticed anything odd about your standoffishness, but he assured us everything was fine and that we just needed to wait for your response from the loan committee. But we knew something was up."

Will then added, "Obviously you've heard the news that Jude was recently fired, but do you know why?"

"All I know is what Jude told me," Frank answered, sounding very nervous. "He called me that night and was extremely upset."

He hesitated for a minute and then, looking at Dan, he said, "Jude told me you were an incompetent leader and wanted him gone because he posed a threat to you."

Charlie spoke up. "Frank, I've worked with basically every personality and ego-driven executive type out there. There's just about nothing I haven't seen or experienced. It's very important that you listen to what I'm about to say.

"Daniel Richards may be young and inexperienced, but what he lacks in experience, he makes up for in heart, intellect, courage, and common sense. He's a smart, talented young man who owns up to his mistakes — as you well know. But I believe he's got what it takes to lead this company to greater success. Will there be struggles on the way? Yes, there will be. But do I believe in him and his abilities? By God, I do.

"And I don't give out compliments lightly. I believe in this young man. And you should, too. Give him a chance. I truly believe he's a natural-born leader."

Will said, "I second that. I'm fully confident in Dan's ability to lead Richards'. He continues to prove himself through his actions to curb nepotism and favoritism. This company is going to go places, and the employees know everyone has to perform or they're out. Hell, I am the COO and was seriously considering retiring until Dan came into the picture. I want to work with this guy!"

Will then looked at Dan and said, "And Dan, I commit to stay with the company for at least the next two years."

"We've also scheduled interviews with two extremely sharp and intelligent CPAs with extensive industry experience," Charlie added. "We expect to fill Jude's position within the next ten days, at which time the new CFO will immediately go to work with our auditing firm and thoroughly investigate what's needed to get all this cleaned up and back on track."

Will then said, "And you need to know the truth about Jude. He was working behind our backs to arrange the sale of this company."

"I thought that was common knowledge!" Frank exclaimed. "You mean you didn't know about the sale, Dan? Jude called me days before that last meeting and told me there were some problems brewing. I wanted to schedule a meeting with you to discuss it, but Jude told me to wait. He told me he had a possible backup in the works with somebody to buy the company just in case. I asked Jude if you knew about this. He told me this potential buyer had just recently approached him and that he intended to sit down with you soon and discuss it.

"That's why I was acting so confused at our last meeting. I did nothing regarding your credit line or anything else because Jude told me to wait — I thought you were planning to sell the company!"

"Then why didn't you say anything in that last meeting?" Dan said, trying to keep his voice under control.

"Because it's just as I told you. Jude asked me not to because he had not yet talked to you!" Frank nearly shouted. He immediately glanced guiltily at Bill.

Bill ignored him, speaking to Dan instead. "I see you've come with documents. What do you have for me?"

With that, Dan presented every report and piece of documentation they had meticulously prepared, going through each line by line. It was a lot, but Dan was surprised at how easily and fluidly the words rolled off his tongue. When he was finished, Bill leaned back in his chair and said, "Well, it looks as though you've done your homework."

"Yes, we have," Dan said. "And trust me, Bill, when I say I'm going to do everything in my power to make sure that Richards' prospers from here on out."

"Well, that's what I like to hear," Bill said. "I still have to take this to the loan committee for final approval, but Dan, I can tell you this bank does not have a problem with this loan."

"Thank you, Bill," Dan said. "This is great news!"

Bill held up a hand. "One more thing," he added. "To avoid any further…problems with this account" — and at that he shot a glance at Frank — "I'll be handling this account personally from here on out."

Charlie and Will looked impressed. "Thank you again," Dan said, shaking Bill's hand. He gathered up the reports, and they filed out of the conference room. Bill walked Dan, Charlie, and Will to the lobby. "One last thing, Dan — sharpen up your golf game! I'll be calling you for a round," he said.

Dan smiled. "I'm looking forward to it," he said.

As Will, Charlie, and Dan walked back to Dan's car, Will was ebullient. "I cannot believe that meeting! We couldn't have asked for a better outcome! I'm impressed, Dan."

"And how did you arrange to have Bill Miller there?" Charlie asked.

Dan told them about their phone conversation that morning. It was a risk calling him, but he knew he had to do it. No guts, no glory, as the saying went.

They got in the car, and Dan turned to them. "I don't know about you two, but I don't have any desire to go back to the office. How does Ducey's sound to you two?"

"You read my mind," Will said. "They have the best margaritas on the planet."

Within 20 minutes, the three of them were sitting in a corner booth with ties loosened, jackets off, and sleeves rolled up. The waitress brought them an ice-cold pitcher of margaritas with three frosted glasses and a basket of hot, fresh tortilla chips, and salsa.

After Charlie had filled everyone's glass, Will raised his in the air. "This has been quite a journey with you two gentlemen, and I would like to make a toast," he said. Charlie and Dan lifted their glasses, too. "To lyin', stealin', cheatin', and drinkin'," Will said. "If you're goin' to lie, lie for a friend. If you're goin' to steal, steal the heart of the one you love. If you're goin' to cheat, cheat death. And if you're goin' to drink, drink with friends. Here's to you, my friends." They clinked glasses, laughing.

As Dan took a long sip, he thought he glimpsed a familiar face out of the corner of his eye. He turned to look, and saw Michelle walking up to their table with a big smile on her face.

"I hope you don't mind if I crash your party!" she said as she slid into the booth. Charlie signaled the waitress for another glass and poured her a margarita. "Will sent me a text asking me to meet you all here. How could I resist an invitation like that?"

"Glad you could make it," said Will. "Dan had quite the coup today during the bank meeting!" He and Charlie began to fill her in on the events of the day.

Dan sat listening to them talk and laugh, reflecting on the ups and downs of the journey that had brought him there. He thought about the first time Will had mentioned bringing in Michelle and Charlie. He had been so concerned about the added cost, given the situation then. Now, considering what that investment had given him and his company, that concern almost made him laugh. Thanksgiving was tomorrow, and Dan thought despite everything, he had a lot to be thankful for.

"You look deep in thought," Michelle said to him, interrupting his reverie. He smiled and took another drink of his margarita. "I was just thinking how I couldn't have gotten even this far without all of you," he said, looking at each one of them. "I know there's still a long road ahead, but — what's that I see? A light at the end of the tunnel?" He shaded his eyes with his hand and squinted into the distance. Charlie, Will, and Michelle laughed.

Then Dan turned to Charlie. "Not to interrupt our celebration with too much serious talk, but you know that long-term I want to take care of our employees. They're the ones who helped build this company.

"Michelle mentioned the other day that you know a thing or two about employee stock ownership plans. When things settle down, I'd like you to tell me more about them."

"I'd love to," Charlie said with a big smile. "But for now, this night is yours, Dan!"

When the waitress reappeared, they ordered enough food to feed three times their party, and spent the next several hours eating, talking, and laughing. At last, a good day.

CHAPTER TWENTY-TWO

THE NEXT MORNING, DAN GOT A CALL FROM Bill Miller. "I have good news," Bill said. "Due to the unique circumstances of your situation, I was able to convene a special gathering of the loan committee right after our meeting. Richards' bank loan is approved and secured."

"That's fantastic!" Dan exclaimed, fighting the urge to dance around his office.

"It was very wise of you to call me yesterday to give me a heads up on things. I respect the way you handled it," Bill continued. "I'd like to give you a little advice for going forward with the bank from here on out. At least once a quarter, give me a full update on what's going on at Richards' — good or bad. We have to be partners, and communication is key.

"If you see a problem coming, pick up the phone and tell me. Don't wait. If you don't understand something, ask. You can see why I appreciate that you called me to share your thoughts about Frank. And I assure you that that situation has been handled.

"And there is one last thing I'd like to tell you. I admire your judgment in how you handled this situation. The bank works with a number of companies where judgment is sadly lacking. And common sense is not always so common. Acquisition of wisdom comes through experience, and experience leads to good judgment. You're on the right track, Dan, and I look forward to the future and building a positive relationship with you and Richards."

As Dan said goodbye and hung up the phone, he felt overwhelmed with relief. He took a deep breath and sat back in his chair. "We did it," he said to himself out loud, smiling.

He went to look for Charlie and Will to tell them news. They were both in Will's office. Dan walked in and closed the door. "Sorry to interrupt your work, but I have some good news and some bad news," he said.

"Oh, no," Will said. "Bad news? What is it, Dan?"

Dan tried to look as serious as he could. "The bad news is… well…there is no bad news!" He broke into a huge smile. "We got the loan! We don't have to sell to Bridger! Bill just called to tell me the news!" Charlie and Will exclaimed so loudly Dan was sure the entire floor could hear them, but he didn't care. This was cause for celebration.

"Congratulations, Dan!" Charlie said, beaming. "This is incredible news!"

Will came around from his desk and shook Dan's hand, then thumped him solidly on the back. Dan had never seen him smile so wide. "I am so proud of you, Dan. You did it," he said.

"No, *we* did it," Dan said. "I couldn't have done any of this without you. You know that. Those 5 Ps of Leadership you told me about that first day I took over Dad's position were exactly right — positive attitude, purpose with determination, planning, patience, and perseverance. I won't forget them."

Turning to Charlie, he said, "Charlie, without your experience, contacts, wisdom, and intuition, we couldn't have done this. You're the one who helped crack everything open. I cannot thank you enough." Charlie shook his hand, still beaming.

"Dan, in a very short time you've proven you're worthy of that office down the hall," Will said. "I'm looking forward to what we can create together. For the first time in a very long time, I'm excited about tomorrow and the future of this place."

Then Charlie added, "And don't forget Michelle. She played a pivotal role from the start with her help and expertise, too, and provided an entirely different perspective that neither Will nor I could have." Dan assured the two men that Michelle was next on his list to inform of the good news.

He had one last thing to cover. "Charlie, I want to talk with you about your ideas for taking this company forward," he said. "Do you have some time today? Our managers' meeting is coming up, and I think this could be part of our overall planning. What do you think?"

"I'd love to, Dan. I need the rest of the morning to finish up some things with Kent, and then we can meet in your office after lunch," Charlie said.

Dan left Will's office practically skipping, he was so happy. He decided to freshen up his coffee and walked into the kitchen. And there they were — Janice, Amy, Nancy, J.D., and Joanne. Only a few months ago he had overheard them lamenting that he was taking over the company. Now they greeted him with genuine warm smiles.

"Good morning, Dan!" Janice said.

Joanne said, "Great to see you this morning!"

"I saw you at the gym last week," Amy chimed in. "You're becoming a regular there again!"

Dan exchanged a few moments of pleasant conversation with them, then poured his coffee and walked back to his office. Things had changed around Richards', and the change reflected in the spirit of the people there. Dan sat down at his desk and picked up the phone to call Michelle. He got her voicemail.

"Hi, Michelle, it's Dan. I have some fantastic news. We got our loan, and things are back on track with the bank. I cannot thank you enough for all you've done for me and for this company.

"You've played an integral role in helping me maneuver through some difficult situations. I needed someone to help me create a plan for my life and find myself again. You've helped me do both, and I honestly believe I wouldn't be where I am now without you. You've kept me grounded and on point. Most of all, you're helping me learn and understand what really matters most in leadership and life. My return on investment has far exceeded my wildest expectations.

"And as far as I'm concerned, my work with you has only begun. I'm looking forward to all that's ahead, and I see you playing a significant role in that future. Thank you again for everything, Michelle. Please call me when you have a minute."

Dan hung up. He had been so wrapped up in resolving things with Jude and the bank that he had endless phone calls and emails to return. But for the first time in a long time, he felt invigorated rather than overwhelmed. The morning passed by in a flash.

Charlie tapped on his office door around 1:00. "Is this a good time?" he asked.

"It sure is. Come in. Have a seat, Charlie."

"So you want to discuss ideas for taking this company forward — perhaps how to get your employees more involved and part of the process," Charlie began. "The number-one thing any organization will say is its biggest issue is developing new leaders. It's not succession planning we're talking about; it's leadership development. People can get the two confused, but they are two very different issues."

Dan said, "I want to be sure I'm building the right foundation for this company around leadership and developing our people. They're our most valuable asset, and I want to begin to put plans in place to allow them to grow professionally as well as financially. I'd like to talk with you about some options for creating a structure that might allow for profit sharing and/ or employee ownership. I hear you know a thing or two about employee stock ownership plans, and I'd like to know more about them." Charlie smiled and nodded.

"Can you give me a basic explanation of what they are and how they work?" Dan asked. "I'm curious to know if a plan like this might someday be beneficial here and for our employees."

"Well, you've come to the right person," Charlie replied. "I was in on the ground floor of the seventh ESOP, which was set up more than forty years ago. I'm an avid believer in ESOPs, and I'll tell you, Dan, that while initially all this might sound complicated, I assure you, as you continue to learn and understand them, you'll see the concept is quite simple and of tremendous financial benefit if created and maintained properly.

"Considering what you've just gone through with your father, an ESOP is something worth considering. ESOPs can be a good way to transition a company and facilitate change of ownership when the time is right. Often, business owners aren't ready to focus on their transition. They don't want to think about it; they're busy with their day-to-day lives, and considering a succession plan or perpetuation planning falls to the bottom of the list. They don't want to have to face their own mortality."

Charlie continued. "I want to be clear that an ESOP is not for every type of business. So let me ask you: In an ideal world, what would you like your company to look like in, say, 20 years?"

Dan thought for a minute. "I'd like to see my employees — the ones who have helped build this company — get the benefit of their hard work," he said. "I want to see Richards' continue to be profitable into the distant future. I'd like to keep the culture of this company and not have to sell when I'm ready to retire. Oh, and most important, I'd like to be able to buy Abby out as soon as possible. She feels the company robbed her of her childhood and her relationship with Dad; getting control of her portion of the business is in both of our best interests."

Charlie nodded. "You just brought up some of the great benefits of an ESOP. But before we get into some of the details of it, let me start with the clinical definition of what an ESOP is. It is a tax-favored vehicle for owners of privately held companies like yours to have an exit strategy that will enable the employees, rather than outside buyers, to acquire stock through a trust. The trust is governed under a body of laws known as ERISA. This is the same body of laws that govern 401(k), profit-sharing, pension, and defined benefit plans.

"Simply put, since Richards' is an S corporation, the ESOP is not subject to federal taxes and can use tax-free profits to buy out existing shareholders. In Abby's case, you could borrow money from the bank to finance the purchase of her stock and pay off the loan with tax-free earnings through the ESOP. Or you could purchase her stock over time through the ESOP with tax-free earnings without having to secure financing.

"An ESOP is the only plan where employees do not have to buy their stock. Over time, employees earn shares based on their financial contribution to the company through their sweat equity. The amount of stock they receive is based on a salary level, which is based on compensation, commissions, and bonuses. Over time every employee in the company will own a piece of Richards', and hopefully they will realize the importance and responsibility of being an employee owner."

Dan nodded, scrawling a few notes as Charlie continued.

"You can imagine what that can do for the morale of your company. I'm involved with the ESOP association, and our studies have shown that the turnover rate for ESOP companies is close to 50 percent lower than non-ESOP companies. We also found that employees in the US who had employee stock ownership were four times less likely to be laid off during the Great Recession than employees without. One of the things I am most proud of is the average account balance among ESOP Association members is close to $200,000."

"How many ESOPs are in existence today in the business world?" Dan asked.

"Great question," Charlie said, "and one I'm proud to answer since I was one of the early ESOP pioneers. There are more than 10,000 active ESOPs covering over 10 million employees. That equates to approximately 10 percent of the private-sector workforce. There would be a lot more if more business leaders and politicians took the time to really understand the benefits of an ESOP. I personally can't think of a better program that works for both sides of the interaction."

"We touched on ESOPs in my MBA program, but I really didn't really understand the benefits," Dan admitted.

Charlie smiled. "Woody Guthrie said, 'Any fool can make something complicated. It takes a genius to make it simple.' I'm no genius, but I do understand ESOPs, and it's very important to get the help of qualified professionals when setting up an ESOP. There's a lot to learn, and we've just skimmed the surface today."

"So where do I begin?" Dan asked.

"You begin with a feasibility study to see if Richards' is a good candidate for implementing an ESOP. But let's not get ahead of ourselves. First, you need to get this company back on its feet and looking to the future. Let's plan on getting back together in a couple of weeks and we can get into more of the details involving the possibility of an ESOP," Charlie said. As he spoke, he glanced at his watch. "I'm sorry to cut this short, but I have another meeting to get to," he said.

"Of course — thank you for your time," Dan said.

After Charlie left, Dan sat for a while, thinking about the responsibility he now had to nurture and protect the future of Richards' and the people who worked for it. He realized, too, that since he took over from his father he had not yet spoken to the entire company. It was high time to call a company meeting, considering all that had happened in these past months. Dan called Georgia and asked her to send out a message to all employees to meet in the large conference room Friday at noon. Dan had some things he needed to say.

CHAPTER TWENTY-THREE

IN THE DAYS LEADING UP TO THE ALL-COMPANY
meeting, Will told Dan he'd heard speculations as to the reason
for the gathering and what Dan was planning to say. Everyone
had heard the news about Jude, and after the shock had worn
off, most people were glad he was gone.

Dan spent a great deal of time thinking about what he was
going to say. In its own way, this talk was going to be another
defining moment in his leadership at Richards'. He was determined to make his mark in the minds and hearts of the entire
company and to tell them that together they would make this
company better than ever.

The day of the presentation, Dan felt a bit nervous, but also
energized. He was looking forward to it. He decided to have
lunch available before his talk, so he asked Georgia to have

everyone arrive around 11:30 instead of noon. As they trickled into the large conference space, Dan tried to personally greet and talk to as many employees as he could. The room was alive with anticipation.

To his surprise, several minutes before he was to take the podium, Will approached him. "I know this is your show, Dan, but would you mind if I introduced you?" he said. "I promise to keep it short. It would mean a lot to me if I could do this." How could Dan refuse such a request?

At exactly noon, Will climbed the three steps to the small stage and took the podium. Dan, standing to the side of the stage, looked out at the hundreds of people seated in the very large room. He noticed Michelle and Charlie standing in the back, and gave them a small wave, glad they could attend. The he noticed another familiar face standing next to Michelle: Bill Miller. He gave Dan a thumbs-up and a smile. Dan smiled back.

"Ladies and gentlemen, could I have your attention, please?" Will said. The room quieted almost immediately.

"It is my great honor to welcome each of you here today. In all my years here with Richards' we've had our share of ups and downs, but nothing matches the challenges we have faced this past year. We all miss Mike. I know I still do. He was my best friend, and a great man who gave everything for this company." Will had to pause a second to hold his composure.

"He is still missed every single day. But his legacy lives on through a young man who, in the past several months, I've gotten to know and respect...and trust.

"Trust is a powerful word. Dan Richards has earned my trust these past months. I believe in him. He has courage and heart.

He is a man of his word. I'm excited to be a part of the new Richards' he is beginning to create.

"Dan has a vision for this company, and it involves each and every one of us. As you will see, this will be a defining moment for this company, as well as for all of you. I promised Dan I would keep this short, so, ladies and gentlemen, I would like to give you our leader and CEO — Dan Richards."

As Will stepped away from the podium, Dan stepped up onto the small stage and looked out over the hundreds of employees clapping and smiling. But he was stunned to see two people walking to the front of the room together.

It can't be, Dan thought. But it was. Grams was heading toward two empty seats in the front row next to Georgia — and with her, arm in arm, was Abby. Dan was momentarily speechless. The clapping had quieted, and he could hear the employees who knew his family greeting his sister and grandmother as they made their way to their seats.

"Well, this is a surprise," Dan began. He looked over at Will, who smiled and shrugged, happy to see that for Dan, it was a good surprise, albeit a momentarily disconcerting one.

"Will, thank you for that introduction. We have been through a lot lately, haven't we? And for those of you who don't know the two lovely ladies who just joined us, let me introduce my beautiful grandmother, Emily Richards, and my sister, Abby. Thank you for being here." Grams gave a little wave as they got settled.

"All of us here, including Grams and Abby, are part of my grandfather's and my father's legacy. And that is what I'd like to talk about — our legacy. As I was preparing this talk today, with the help of our human resources team, I was able to find some amazing statistics. More than 55 percent of all of you sitting here today have parents who are currently working here or who have worked here. One out of three of you have relatives who worked for my grandfather." He smiled at John and Eldon Savage in the audience.

"This organization was built on hard work, dedication, and commitment. But there is another component that went into the success of this company. It's family." Dan looked at Grams and Abby.

"I believe we are a family here. And as you all know, families have their fair share of ups and downs, but if they're committed to each other and staying together, they survive. And to me, Richards' is a family.

"I want each and every one of you here today to know my commitment to you and to this company. As sure as I'm standing here in front of you, I am going to make mistakes along the way. I have a lot to learn and some very big shoes to fill. But I commit to you that I will do whatever it takes to keep Richards' growing and thriving. I commit to do my best to serve you, our customers, and this company.

"But I'm going to need your help. I'm going to need the help of every one of you here in this room. I'm asking you for your continued loyalty, hard work, and dedication.

"I believe when people are part of the process they're part of the outcome. So I ask that you come to Will or me with your ideas and suggestions for making our company better. It's my hope that you come to work here because you want to, not because you have to. I want this company to have a contagious spirit of enjoyment and satisfaction that our customers can feel each time they visit us.

"We have family members and friends working side by side here, and although it's nice to work together, that can create its own set of challenges. I hope you have noticed by the recent adjustments that have been made since I have taken over that this company will be built on fairness, honesty, and equality, not entitlement. Hard work and success will be rewarded, and anything less than that will have consequences.

"Not too long ago I read a quote my grandfather had saved by Henry Ford that said, 'Coming together is the beginning. Keeping together is progress. Working together is success.' I believe this quote is as appropriate now as it was when Grandfather cut it out of the newspaper all those years ago.

"This company was originally built on the principles of strong family values, honesty, humility, respect, courage, determination and dedication, common sense, and loyalty. It is my goal to continue to grow and develop each of these core principles here.

"It is also my goal that years from now when I step down from this position and the next person takes over, perhaps my son or daughter, or maybe one of yours — " Dan glanced at Abby, who was watching him intently — "that he or she inherits a strong and thriving company that was built on all these principles. I want your children to inherit and reap the positive benefits of the seeds we are sowing together. This deeply valued and cherished legacy has been left to each of us.

"I have only started researching and understanding a way for each of you to possibly share in the success of this company and how you can become partners in its success. In time I'll be telling you more about it. But for now I want you to know I am committed to you and this company just as my father and grandfather were.

"I would like to close by telling you about a Rudyard Kipling poem my grandfather lived by. It helped him through the ups and downs of life and it continues to help me, too. Grams, you told me he memorized this, and so I did, too." Dan looked at her and saw her brushing a tear from her cheek. Abby was holding her other hand.

"The name of the poem is 'If,'" Dan said. He could see Grams beaming from the corner of his field of vision as he began to recite:

> *If you can keep your head when all about you*
> *Are losing theirs and blaming it on you,*
> *If you can trust yourself when all men doubt you*
> *But make allowance for their doubting too,*
> *If you can wait and not be tired by waiting,*
> *Or being lied about, don't deal in lies,*
> *Or being hated, don't give way to hating,*
> *And yet don't look too good, nor talk too wise:*

> *If you can dream — and not make dreams your master,*
> *If you can think — and not make thoughts your aim;*
> *If you can meet with Triumph and Disaster*
> *And treat those two impostors just the same;*
> *If you can bear to hear the truth you've spoken*
> *Twisted by knaves to make a trap for fools,*
> *Or watch the things you gave your life to, broken,*
> *And stoop and build 'em up with worn-out tools:*

If you can make one heap of all your winnings
And risk it on one turn of pitch-and-toss,
And lose, and start again at your beginnings
And never breathe a word about your loss;
If you can force your heart and nerve and sinew
To serve your turn long after they are gone,
And so hold on when there is nothing in you
Except the Will which says to them: "Hold on!"

If you can talk with crowds and keep your virtue,
Or walk with kings — nor lose the common touch,
If neither foes nor loving friends can hurt you;
If all men count with you, but none too much,
If you can fill the unforgiving minute
With sixty seconds' worth of distance run,
Yours is the Earth and everything that's in it,
And — which is more — you'll be a Man, my son!

Dan paused for a brief moment remembering his Dad and Grandfather. Then he said, "I want to thank all of you for everything you have given to my dad and to Richards'. And I want to thank you for your continued support, patience, and belief in me, and in our company — our family."

As he left the stage and walked toward Abby and Grams, people rose from their chairs as they clapped. Dan felt like a cycle had been completed — from grandfather to father to son — and it wouldn't have been nearly as satisfying without the rest of his family there. Grams hugged him for a long time, squeezing him with all her strength. Then he turned to Abby.

"I'm very proud of you, Dan," Abby said with a tentative smile. "When Will called and told me about the company-wide speech, I booked a flight immediately. I arrived last night, and I'm really glad I decided to come."

"I'm glad, too," Dan said, as they hugged.

He wanted to talk to Grams and Abby longer, but a line was forming of employees wanting to shake his hand and comment on his speech, and Abby signaled that they'd meet him later. As great as it was to hear that people felt reassured and confident in him, he couldn't shake the thought that something was still missing. That had one more person been there, the moment would have been even more satisfying. He did his best not to think of Julie.

CHAPTER TWENTY-FOUR

SPRING HAD FINALLY ARRIVED, AND DAN decided to take his workout regimen outdoors. He and Mully were now up to running four or five miles every morning. But since it was the weekend, he decided to treat himself to a few extra hours of sleep before their run.

As he tried to tie the laces of his running shoes, Mully jumped all over him, panting, excited for their late morning run. Dan attached her leash, and they took off down the driveway toward the park.

The sun was bright and warm, and the spring flowers were just beginning to bud. The air was fragrant and it was a beautiful day.

Dan had not gotten very far down the running trail at the park when his shoelace became untied and he had to stop. As he bent down to tie it, he saw someone jogging toward him. She was tall with a long brunette ponytail and, from the looks of it, was in very good shape. She got closer, and Dan froze. She had headphones on and appeared to be in another world — but as she neared Dan she noticed him and began to slow.

"Hi," she said, stopping in front of him and trying to catch her breath. "I didn't expect to see you here."

Dan stood up quickly, his shoelace still untied. "I didn't expect to see you here, either. It's good to see you, Julie."

They stood nervously looking at each other for a few seconds. Julie was slightly flushed from her run and looked better than ever; Dan felt the same butterflies he'd experienced the first time he saw her. He was just about to open his mouth, still unsure of what exactly to say, when Mully saved him by nudging Julie's leg, wanting some attention.

"Oh, hello, sweet girl," Julie said, bending down to pet her. Mully's tail wagged a mile a minute, and she kept trying to lick Julie's face, making her laugh.

"She's adorable, Dan. I didn't know you'd gotten a dog. When did you get her?"

"About a year ago," Dan said carefully. Julie glanced up at him, then went back to petting Mully. "She's beautiful, and so sweet. What's your name, sweet girl?" she said.

"Her name is Mulligan," Dan said. "I call her Mully for short."

"Mulligan? That's an interesting name for a dog. Why did you name her that?" Julie asked, smiling and scratching between Mully's ears.

Dan paused for a second. Then he said, "Because Mulligan... means getting a second chance."

Julie stopped petting Mully and looked up at him again, flashing him that familiar smile.

Dan thought about what Michelle had taught him about taking risks and envisioning positive outcomes, and knew he had to go for it. "Julie, how would you like to get a cup of coffee with Mully and me?" he said, stumbling just a little over his words. "It's a gorgeous day and we could sit outside…"

Julie interrupted him. "I was actually just about to ask you the same thing!" she said.

Dan's heart soared. He remembered what Julie used to tell him: "If you want something bad enough, the universe will conspire in every way to make it happen."

He now understood exactly what that meant as they walked together out of the park toward the coffee shop: Dan with Julie…and his Mulligan.

DICKSON C. BUXTON, Chartered Financial Consultant, co-founded Private Capital Corporation (PCC) in 1976 and was Chairman of the PCC Kelso subsidiary from 1978-1981.

As Co-founder of the ESOP Association of America, he conducted the first major ESOP productivity study for the Senate Finance Committee in 1979. Dick and his associates have designed over 1,000 exit and succession plans over the last four decades. Management Stock Ownership Plans and, where appropriate, ESOP's were included.

PCC created the first ESOP oriented Private Equity Group in 1979. Dick was co-founder in 1987 of MBR Investment Associates, a Private Equity Group for mid-market companies.

Buxton is the author of several successful business books: *You've Built A Successful Business—Now What?* in 1996, and *Lessons in Leadership and Life—Secrets of Eleven Wise Men*, in 2002.

To learn more about Dick and Private Capital Corporation, please visit www.PrivateCapitalCorp.com or find Dick at LinkedIn/in/DicksonBuxton.

DIANE LUDGATE LOVE, PhD, is founder and president of Successful Solutions, a business specializing in executive coaching and organizational training. As an executive coach, corporate trainer, and keynote speaker, Diane has worked with hundreds of senior and mid-level executives in organizations ranging from Fortune 500 and mid-size companies to start-ups and nonprofits.

Diane has worked with business professionals throughout North America, the UK, and India. Her extensive 20-year corporate management background along with her academic achievements makes her a one-of-kind professional. She is an accomplished entrepreneur, and prior to founding Successful Solutions, Diane started her career working at Dayton Hudson Corporation (now Macy's Inc.) and then on to Steelcase, Inc.

She exudes passion, optimism, and a genuine belief that all things are possible with confidence, commitment, and inspired action.

To learn more about Diane and Successful Solutions,
please visit www.MySuccessfulSolutions.com
or find Diane at LinkedIn/in/DianeLudgateLove.

www.ingramcontent.com/pod-product-compliance
Lightning Source LLC
Chambersburg PA
CBHW050504210326
41521CB00011B/2314